THE
ULTIMATE
ALLERGY-FREE
SNACK
COOKBOOK

OVER 100 KID-FRIENDLY RECIPES
FOR THE ALLERGIC CHILD

JUDI AND SHARI ZUCKER

SQUAREONE
PUBLISHERS

COVER DESIGNER: Jeannie Tudor
COVER PHOTO: Getty Images, Inc.
EDITOR: Marie Caratozzolo
TYPESETTER: Theresa E. Wiscovitch
INTERIOR ART: Cathy Morrison

Square One Publishers
115 Herricks Road
Garden City Park, NY 11040
(516) 535-2010 • (877) 900-BOOK
www.squareonepublishers.com

Library of Congress Cataloging-in-Publication Data
Zucker, Judi.
    The ultimate allergy-free snack cookbook: over 100 kid-friendly recipes
for the allergic child / Judi and Shari Zucker.
        p. cm.
    Includes index.
    ISBN 978-0-7570-0346-2 (pbk.)
1. Food allergy—Diet therapy—Recipes. 2. Cookbooks. I. Zucker, Shari. II.
Title.
    RC588.D53Z83 2012
    641.56318—dc23
                                                                    2011037532

Printed in the United States of America

10   9   8   7   6   5   4   3   2

CONTENTS

We would like to dedicate this book to our dear friend
Mardi Warkentin.
When faced with a difficult health diagnosis,
Mardi educated herself, changed her diet, and stayed positive.
She is now healthier than ever—
a true inspiration!

ACKNOWLEDGMENTS

Together, we would like to thank publisher Rudy Shur, founder of Square One Publishers, for believing in this project and supporting our commitment to educate others on the benefits of a healthful lifestyle. His guidance and expertise were invaluable. Rudy taught us that when you think you have given your very best, you can still do better.

We are also very thankful to our editor, Marie Caratozzolo. Her organizational abilities and attention to detail really helped this book take shape. She is the best editor we have ever had.

For their input on this project, we would also like to acknowledge Anna Ylvisaker, Richard and Claudia Handin, and Lucia Engel, as well as Joanne Abrams, Colleen Day, Shoshana Shapiro, Erica Shur, Lesley Steinberg, Michael Weatherhead, and Stephanie Zeitlin.

A special word of gratitude goes to noted vegan chef Vicki Chelf, who created the recipe for the Mini Crunch Cups (page 44) specifically for this book.

Finally, we must extend heartfelt thanks to our parents, Irwin and Devra Zucker, and our sister, Lori Zucker, for their never-ending love and support.

I would like to thank my husband, Chris, and our children, Taryn and Tanner, for their love (and for being such great taste-testers). It is also a blessing to be a twin. Shari is my built-in cheerleader. Together we share a passion for good health and nutrition. It is a joy having her as a writing partner.

Judi

To my husband, Daniel, and to our three children—Maxwell, Miles, and Mattea—thank you for your love and compassion, and for keeping me smiling every day. And to Judi, thanks for being the best writing partner ever! Being a twin is awesome!

Shari

FOREWORD

As an emergency medicine physician for over thirty years, I have seen thousands of patients and treated my fair share of medical emergencies, ranging from burns and broken bones to heart attacks and strokes. In many of these cases, carelessness, miscalculations, and even ignorance have been the cause. In addition, many of the life-threatening conditions I treat are the result of poor dietary choices coupled with unhealthy lifestyles. I have seen firsthand how diets that are filled with saturated fat, sugar, and processed foods can take a toll on good health. In my opinion, with a little precaution, the number of people passing through our emergency departments and hospitals could be cut down considerably.

Through my work, I have also witnessed a significant rise in the number of emergency department cases involving food allergies, particularly among children. For anyone with food allergies, when it comes to diet, avoiding the allergenic substance is paramount; however, the importance of eating a healthy diet is just as important for maintaining overall good health.

Authors Judi and Shari Zucker are strong believers in the connection between good health and nutritious dietary habits. In their latest work *The Ultimate Allergy-Free Snack Cookbook,* they present a treasure trove of recipes for delicious, satisfying snacks for kids that are free from the eight most common food allergens. While the authors recognize that there are hundreds of non-allergenic snacks that parents can buy for their children, they also realize that many are processed and loaded with unhealthy ingredients like sugar, food colorings, flavor enhancers, and preservatives. To this end, their snacks are made with healthful unprocessed (or minimally processed) natural ingredients.

What makes this work stand apart from other cookbooks of this type is that it offers much more than simply recipes. It provides parents with a clear understanding of food allergies and how they differ from food intolerances. It also explains how to recognize allergenic ingredients on product labels, while offering safe ingredient substitutions for the offending foods. The importance of healthy eating, which I heartily applaud, is strongly emphasized. When children form good eating habits early on, they will continue to carry them throughout their lives.

Yes, I've seen adults in the ER who have had allergic reactions to foods they've mistakenly ingested; however, I see more adults who have had heart attacks, strokes, diabetic complications, and a host of other serious conditions resulting from a lifetime of poor dietary choices. With this book, you can help teach your children how to successfully avoid foods to which they are allergic, as wellas guide them in making the right food choices for good health—so they never have to see the inside of an emergency room. With a little precaution today, they can avoid many health problems tomorrow. It can all begin with this important book.

Richard F. Handin, MD
Diplomate American Board of Emergency Medicine
Fellow of the American College
of Emergency Physicians

INTRODUCTION

There is no question that the number of children developing food allergies is growing, and strict avoidance of the offending food is the only way to prevent a reaction. This increase in food allergies has given rise to a growing number of commercial products that are becoming readily available on store shelves. Initially, this may appear to be a good thing. The problem is that while these products may be allergen-free, they are often short on nutrition. Commercially made crackers, chips, trail mixes, energy bars, cookies, and other baked goods tend to be highly processed and loaded with sugar, salt, trans fats, preservatives, food colorings, and other undesirable ingredients. So what's the solution? How can you provide your child with snacks that are not only appealing, but also nutritionally sound?

The Ultimate Allergy-Free Snack Cookbook is designed to help. It provides over 100 vegetarian recipes that are free of eggs, cow's milk, soy, wheat, peanuts, tree nuts, fish, and shellfish—the most common allergenic foods according to the current assessment of the U.S. Food and Drug Administration. The recipes are also free of gluten and refined white sugar. As an added bonus, the snacks are wholesome, natural, and nutritious—high in whole grains, rich in fiber, and low in calories. Best of all, they are simple to make. In fact, you'll be delighted to see just how easy it is to prepare tantalizing snacks that fill kids up in a healthy way.

Of course, even the most nutritious foods won't benefit your kids unless they eat them. That's why the following chapters are jam packed with kid-favorite snack choices—cookies, muffins, brownies, chips, dips, pizza, puddings, mini burgers, sorbets, smoothies, and more. But this book is not just about recipes. It also offers helpful information and support for anyone living with an allergic family. There are guidelines for setting up an allergen-free kitchen, instructions on how to read food labels, and tips for avoiding cross-contamination of allergenic ingredients. A comprehensive table provides ingredient options for a number of common food allergens. With it, you can easily adjust most recipes to suit the particular needs of your child. Peppered throughout the book you'll find a number of "Just for Fun" entries. These entries cover a variety of snack-time subjects, such as creative ways to serve snacks, ideas for party snacks, and kid-involved "snack-tivities" that any child is sure to enjoy. This really is the ultimate snack cookbook!

It doesn't matter if the snackin' good choices in this book are enjoyed as lunchbox goodies, after-school treats, or party fare, your child is going to look forward to all of them. And it does not matter which of the top allergenic foods affect your child, nor does it matter if the allergy is mild or severe—he or she can enjoy *all* of the snacks in this book without fear of a reaction. Low in fat and calories, yet high in flavor, these snacks are not just for kids with allergies. Everyone can enjoy them!

1

Food Allergies—A Growing Concern

Over 12 million people in the United States suffer from food allergies, and the highest incidence is among children under the age of eighteen. According to a study published in the journal *Pediatrics*, between 1997 and 2007, pediatric food allergies increased by 18 percent! *The Journal of Allergy and Clinical Immunology* recently reported that between 2001 and 2006, visits to the Children's Hospital Boston emergency room due to allergic reactions more than doubled. Many hospitals throughout the United States are reporting similar statistics.

Heredity is believed to be the primary cause of allergies. Chances are one in three that a child will develop an allergy if one parent has an allergy of any type. These odds increase to seven in ten if both parents have allergies. But why the sudden increase?

A growing number of researchers suggest that the noticeable rise in children's allergies may be due to what is called the *hygiene hypothesis*—our tendency toward "clean living." We strive for an antiseptic, dirt-free world; one in which our immune systems no longer have to fight germs the way they used to. Medications and antibiotics have taken further burden off our immune systems, which have shifted their focus from fighting infections to developing more allergic tendencies, such as viewing harmless proteins in foods as harmful invaders, overreacting to them, and then causing an allergic response. Since more people are developing allergies and more allergic couples are having children, the increase in the number of affected children is naturally on the rise.

Some researchers believe that introducing certain known allergenic foods into a child's diet too early may be another cause of the rising allergy rates—a theory that has proven controversial. And recently, another interesting study conducted at Italy's University of Florence indicated that poor dietary choices, such as those associated with the Western diet, may also be a contributing factor to a child's susceptibility to allergies, as well as obesity and a number of other conditions and illnesses. Researchers compared the effects of the fiber-rich diet of fourteen children from a rural African village in Burkina Faso to the more-

Westernized diets of fifteen children from Florence. The African children ate mostly grains, beans, nuts, and vegetables that had been raised near their homes, while the diet of the Italian children included more meat, fat, and sugar.

Study results showed that the digestive systems of the African children were flourishing with "good" bacteria and an abundance of beneficial fatty acids, which are associated with a reduced risk of obesity, inflammation, asthma, eczema, and other allergic reactions. By comparison, the systems of the Italian children had nowhere near the same beneficial environment—a condition that could lead to allergies and other inflammatory diseases.

There is no question that the number of children developing food allergies is growing. While strict avoidance of the offending food may be the only way to prevent a reaction, eating a healthy, nutritious diet may be another important factor in reducing the risk that can lead to allergies.

UNDERSTANDING ALLERGIES

What exactly is a food allergy? Is it the same as food intolerance? Although both involve food sensitivities, these two conditions are different.

A *food allergy* occurs when the body's immune system overreacts to a food, believing it is harmful. To protect itself, the immune system mistakenly produces antibodies called *immunoglobulin E* (IgE). These antibodies then cause the body to generate chemicals called *histamines*, which can cause an allergic response. This response can range from minor skin irritations like an itchy rash or stuffy nose to more serious respiratory problems, including life-threatening *anaphylaxis*. Signs of anaphylaxis, which usually occur within minutes after exposure to the allergen, typically include difficulty breathing and swallowing, and swelling of the lips, tongue, and throat. Early administration of epinephrine (available in an injectable "pen") is critical for successful treatment.

A *food intolerance* is similar to an allergy in that it causes an adverse reaction to a food; but unlike an allergy, it does not involve the immune system. Symptoms of food intolerance—often headaches and digestive issues—also tend to be less severe and non-life threatening. Although many foods can cause an intolerance, the most common offenders include *lactose*, a sugar found in milk and most dairy products; *salicylates*, a natural chemical contained in a variety of fruits and vegetables; *amines*, a chemical produced during the fermentation of wine and the ripening of certain foods; and *glutamate*, an amino acid in foods containing protein. The popular flavor enhancer monosodium glutamate (MSG) is the sodium salt of glutamate and a common cause of sensitivity.

Celiac disease, also known as *gluten intolerance*, is a digestive condition that, although not considered an allergy, involves an immune system response. For a person with celiac, antibodies attack the lining of the small intestine when gluten is present. The lining becomes inflamed and is unable to absorb nutrients and minerals from food. A gluten-free diet—avoidance of all products containing wheat, rye, spelt, kamut, and barley—is the only treatment for this condition.

Food allergies are more common in children than adults. The good news is that the majority of affected children outgrow them with age.

OFFENDING FOODS

Unlike many non-food allergies, which can be treated with medication, there is no cure for food allergies. Strict avoidance of the offending food is the only way to prevent a reaction. The eight foods that trigger most allergic responses are

FOOD ALLERGY PRECAUTIONS

If your child has a food allergy—especially a severe allergy—there are some precautions you can take to prevent potential problems.

✔ Be sure to alert everyone your child comes in contact with—teachers, school cafeteria staff, servers at restaurants, parents of playmates, babysitters—about his or her allergy.

✔ It is best to prepare your child's meals at home, where you are certain of the ingredients.

✔ Make allergen-free snacks and treats for your child to take to parties and play dates.

✔ If you don't know ALL of the ingredients in a prepared food or food product, do not serve it to your child.

✔ If possible, do not keep the problem food in the home.

✔ Read food labels carefully for the presence of allergens. (See the table on page 10.) Some food manufacturers label their products to verify that they were prepared or packed in an allergen-free (or non allergen-free) environment. If there is any question regarding the possibility of a product's cross-contact with an allergenic food, contact the manufacturer directly.

✔ If you keep the allergen food in your home, be careful of cross-contamination. Don't use the same utensils, cookware, cutting boards, etc. to prepare allergenic and non-allergenic foods. At places like ice cream parlors, be cautious of cross-contact that can result from shared scoops.

✔ In cases of severe allergies, keep epinephrine (EpiPen, Twinject) accessible at all times.

peanuts, tree nuts, cow's milk and other dairy products, eggs, wheat, soy, fish, and crustacean shellfish. Children are more likely to suffer from allergies due to milk, eggs, and peanuts, while adults tend to be more allergic to fish and shellfish. Let's take a closer look at these highly allergenic foods—none of which are contained in the recipes in this book.

Peanuts

Actually legumes (not nuts), peanuts are a growing cause of allergic reactions in children. According to a recent survey that appeared in *The Journal of Allergy and Clinical Immunology*, the number of children with peanut allergies more than tripled between 1997 and 2008. Nearly half of these children are also allergic to tree nuts. For many, a peanut allergy is a lifelong concern—only about 20 percent of children outgrow it.

An allergic reaction to peanuts can be mild or severe depending on the sensitivity of the individual. Even an extremely small amount can cause serious life-threatening anaphylaxis in some people.

It is obvious that peanut butter and any food or product that includes the word "peanut" indicates that it contains peanut protein, making the product easy to avoid. Sometimes, however, peanuts are sold as "beer nuts" or "monkey nuts," which are not as obvious. It is very important to read food labels to determine if the product contains peanut protein, which can be found in a number of unlikely sources. (See "Guide to Avoiding Food Allergens" beginning on page 10.)

Tree Nuts

Approximately 1 percent of children in North America are allergic to tree nuts. Brazil nuts almonds, cashews, chestnuts, walnuts, pecans, hazelnuts, macadamias, pistachios, and pine nuts are common tree nut varieties, but they are not the only ones.

Allergic reactions to tree nuts, as with peanuts, are generally lifelong and can be severe and even life-threatening. For the most part, people who are allergic to one tree nut are not usually allergic to *all* varieties. They may, however, be allergic to one or even a few others. They are also at greater risk for developing peanut allergies. For this reason—as well as the possibility of cross-contamination during the manufacturing process—most doctors advise that if your child is allergic to one tree nut, it is best to simply avoid all nuts, and peanuts, too.

What about coconuts? Although the FDA considers coconut to be a tree nut (for food labeling purposes), technically, it is a seed, not a nut. Coconut allergies are actually very rare—most people with tree nut allergies are able to eat coconut without having an adverse reaction. So before eliminating coconut from your child's diet, first discuss this possibility with your doctor.

Also keep in mind that although chestnuts fall into the tree nut category, water chestnuts do not. Water chestnuts are the edible portion of a plant root, and safe for anyone with tree nut allergies. Nutmeg is also safe. Although it includes the word "nut" in its name, nutmeg is actually the fragrant seed of a tropical tree.

Like peanuts, many foods that contain tree nuts are obvious, but there are many unexpected sources as well. A growing number of commercial products like salad dressings, cereals, meatless burgers, and pie crusts contain tree nuts. And many ethnic cuisines, such as Greek and Chinese, are famous for dishes and pastries that contain nuts. Reading food labels and maintaining an awareness of the possible presence of food allergens in unexpected sources is critical. For details, see the listing on page 11.

Milk

An allergy to cow's milk is the most common childhood food allergy, affecting approximately 2.5 percent of children under age three. Most affected children develop the allergy during their first year. *Casein*, the protein in cow's milk is the most common culprit, although most children who are allergic to cow's milk are also allergic to goat's milk and sheep's milk. Some are also allergic to soymilk.

Typical symptoms of a milk allergy, which usually occur shortly after consumption, include vomiting, hives, and gastrointestinal distress. These reactions can be mild or severe, although generally they are not life threatening. On a positive note, many children outgrow milk allergies by the time they are three or four years old. By age eighteen, most are no longer affected.

Along with cheese, butter, yogurt, and ice cream, milk is found in a tremendous number of processed foods and baked goods. When checking ingredient labels, keep an eye out for the words "whey" and "casein," which indicate "milk." There are many other foods that may contain milk or other dairy products and must be avoided (see the list on page 12).

If your child has a milk allergy, be especially careful when eating in Mexican or Italian restaurants, where cheese is a popular ingredient and could possibly cross-contaminate your child's food. And be careful at delis, where cold cuts may be cut on the same slicer that is used for cheese. Also be aware that lactose-free milks and other lactose-free products still contain milk solids and are not meant for anyone with a milk allergy. They are intended for those who are lactose intolerant.

Eggs

An egg allergy follows milk as the second most-common childhood food allergy. Affecting over 1.5 percent of children, an egg allergy usually begins when a child is very young, and is often gone by age seven or eight. The allergic reaction (more often to the egg white than the yolk) usually starts within minutes or hours after eating eggs and doesn't last more than a day. Typical reactions include hives or skin rash, runny nose, sneezing, watery eyes, coughing, breathing difficulties, vomiting, and diarrhea. Most children will experience more than one of these reactions, which could be mild or severe. In very rare cases, life-threatening anaphylaxis can occur.

Eggs aren't just found in omelets. They are contained in many prepared foods, baked goods, and processed products. And don't be fooled into thinking that commercial egg substitutes found in the refrigerated section of your grocery store are egg-free. Most contain egg whites. There are, however, a few vegan egg-free substitutes that come in powdered form and are safe to use.

It's important to be aware of the many hidden egg sources—like pretzels, dinner rolls, and loaves of bread, which are sometimes coated with egg wash for a glossy shine, or that cappuccino, whose foamy topping may contain egg. Check the listing on page 13 for other foods and ingredients to avoid.

Wheat

Another common childhood food allergy is caused by the protein found in wheat. This allergy usually develops when a child is between six months and two years old. Most children outgrow it by age five. Like many allergic reactions, symptoms of wheat allergy usually occur a few minutes to a few hours after eating the problem food. Typical symptoms, which can be mild or severe, include hives, itchy eyes, difficulty breathing, nausea or vomiting, and diarrhea. In some severe cases, anaphylaxis can occur.

Children with a wheat allergy must avoid all products made from wheat. It is important that they also stay away from products made from spelt and kamut—two grains that are related to wheat. (For a detailed list of these products, see page 14.) They are, however, able to eat other grains, such as amaranth, barley, corn, oats, quinoa, rice, and rye.

A wheat allergy is sometimes confused with celiac disease—also called *gluten intolerance*. As mentioned earlier, those with celiac disease cannot eat *any* product that contains gluten, which is found not only in wheat but also in rye, kamut, spelt, and barley. Unlike a wheat allergy, which is often outgrown, celiac disease is a lifelong condition and, unfortunately, the number of people who have it is on the rise. Although it is not considered an allergy, celiac disease does involve an immune system response that targets and damages the lining of the small intestine. For this reason, the recipes in this book—in addition to being free of the eight top food allergens—are also gluten-free, which makes them safe for those with celiac disease.

Soy

Like peanuts, soybeans are classified as legumes. Childhood allergies to soybeans and soy products are about half as common as peanut allergies. In infants, rashes and digestive problems are often signs of a soy allergy, while toddlers and older children tend to experience runny nose, watery eyes, wheezing, and other cold-like symptoms. These allergic reactions are generally mild in nature; however, anaphylaxis can occur in rare cases. Although most children eventually outgrow a soy allergy by age ten, for some, it continues into adulthood.

Because soybeans are so inexpensive, a growing number of food manufacturers have begun replacing more costly ingredients with soy products. For instance, the peanut oil once used in many brands of peanut butter has been replaced with cheaper vegetable oil blends that often contain soy oil. Some herbal teas contain soy as a filler. And even fresh produce is sometimes sprayed with soy oil to give it an eye-appealing shine. (Buying certified organic produce is one way to avoid this particular problem.)

Seafood, Fish and Shellfish

Seafood allergies affect approximately 7 million Americans. Although this type of allergy is more common in adults than children, it can occur at any age; and for most, it is a lifelong condition. Allergic reactions usually begin a few minutes to a few hours after consuming the food, and may include dizziness; tingling or swelling of the lips, tongue, or throat; itching; hives; difficulty breathing; nausea; and diarrhea. A severe reaction can cause anaphylaxis.

Salmon, tuna, and halibut are among the fish (with fins and backbones) that are considered the most allergenic. As for shellfish, which fall into two categories—crustaceans and mollusks—only crustaceans are considered major food allergens. Shrimp, lobster, and crab are among the top offenders. Because mollusks, such as clams, oysters, and scallops, are not considered major allergens, they do not have to be listed on ingredient labels. (See "Food Labeling" on the next page for more information.) If your child is allergic to crustacean shellfish, the doctor may advise that he or she avoid mollusks as well. (An extensive list appears in the "Guide to Avoiding Food Allergens" beginning on page 16.)

In addition to reading ingredient labels and knowing which foods to avoid, it is also a good idea to steer clear of seafood restaurants, where cross-contamination can easily involve a non-fish dish. And watch out for fried foods—many restaurants use the same oil to fry both seafood and non-seafood dishes. It is also important to be aware that Asian restaurants often flavor their dishes with fish-based sauces, so be very careful when ordering.

The only way to prevent your child from having an allergic food reaction is simply to avoid the problem food. Obviously, it is important to be aware of these foods and ingredients, which are sometimes "hidden" under unfamiliar names or sources on food labels.

FOOD LABELING

On January 1, 2006, the Food Allergen Labeling and Consumer Protection Act (FALCPA) took effect. This act requires that foods containing one or more major food allergen (milk, eggs, peanuts, tree nuts, soy, wheat, fish, and crustacean shellfish) must state the allergen in plain language on the label.

The specific allergen may appear on the ingredient list or it may be stated in parentheses after the listed food source, for example "albumin (egg)." It may also appear in a section near the ingredient list after the word "contains" (e.g. "Contains soy and wheat."). These allergens must be listed if they are present in any amount, and if they are in spice blends, colorings, flavorings, preservatives, or any other additives. Additionally, manufacturers must list the *specific* nut (e.g. almonds, macadamia nuts, walnuts) or seafood (e.g., salmon, shrimp, lobster) that is contained in the product.

FALCPA has certainly made label reading easier for the millions of Americans living with food allergies. Be aware, however, that *these requirements do not cover all foods*. For instance, packaged take-out food from restaurants, fast-food establishments, and street vendors that is provided in response to a person's order, is not required to follow FALCPA guidelines. This is also the case for prepared foods sold in grocery stores and delis. Other products that are not covered by FALCPA include fresh fruits and vegetables, highly refined oils, and beer and other alcoholic beverages.

Kosher products are also exempt from FALCPA guidelines. And keep in mind that locally made and distributed foods may not be in full compliance. It is also very important to remember that these labeling requirements are for American food products only—foods that are packaged in Canada and other countries are not required to list allergens as clearly (or at all). An allergen such as soy, for example, may be contained in a product, yet "hidden" under an ingredient such as "natural flavors." The message here is clear: *Always* check labels carefully for food allergens, including those that are possibly "hidden." (See the "Guide to Avoiding Food Allergens" beginning on page 10.) If you are not 100-percent certain of the ingredients in a product, do not give it to your child.

CROSS-CONTAMINATION CONCERNS

Thanks to the FALCPA, food manufacturers must clearly state in plain English the presence of any of the top allergenic foods on product labels. Currently, however, manufacturers are *not* required to state if the food was processed in a facility that processes other allergenic foods—where the possibility of cross-contamination is a real concern.

Fortunately, although they are not required to do so, a growing number of manufacturers are voluntarily including this information on labels. The note can state, for example, that the product was made in a "wheat-free" or "dairy-free" facility. Or, as a warning, it can say that the product "may contain wheat" or that it was "processed in a facility that also processes peanuts."

When checking ingredient lists, be sure to also look for this additional note. If there isn't one, don't assume the product is safe. If there is any question regarding the possibility of a product's cross-contact with an allergenic food, contact the manufacturer directly.

Guide to Avoiding Food Allergens

The following table presents the eight common food allergens along with many of the foods, products, and ingredients that may cause an allergic reaction. As discussed in the section on "Food Labeling" (page 9), most—*but not all*—foods packaged in the United States must clearly state if the product contains any of these allergens. *Always check food labels carefully.* And be aware that manufacturers often change product ingredients suddenly and without notice, so never skip reading labels of familiar products because you "know" what they contain. It is important to check labels with every purchase.

Peanuts

FOODS/ INGREDIENTS TO AVOID	Anything with the word "peanut" (brittle, butter, etc.)		
	Arachis	Goober peas	Monkey nuts
	Arachis hypogaea	Goobers	Nu-Nuts
	Arachis oil	Ground nuts	Nut pieces
	Artificial nuts	Hydrolyzed peanut protein	Nutmeat
	Beer nuts	Hypogaeic acid	Peanut oil (cold-pressed, expeller-pressed, extruded)
	Crushed nuts	Mandelonas	
	Earth nuts	Mixed nuts	

MAY CONTAIN PEANUT PROTEIN	Artificial and natural flavorings
	Baked goods (cookies, cakes, pastries, breads)
	Ethnic foods/dishes: African, Asian, Mexican, and especially Chinese, Indian, Indonesian, Thai, and Vietnamese

MAY CONTAIN PEANUT PROTEIN (cont.)	Candy	Fried foods	Marzipan
	Chili	Granola bars	Mole sauce
	Chocolate	Hydrolyzed plant protein	Nougat
	Crumb/streusel toppings	Hydrolyzed vegetable protein	Pie crusts
	Egg rolls		Trail mixes
	Enchilada sauce		

IMPORTANT INFORMATION	* According to the FDA, studies have shown that most allergic individuals can eat purified or highly refined peanut oil (not cold-pressed, extruded, or expeller-pressed) without a reaction. *Always check with your child's doctor first.*

Tree Nuts

FOODS/ INGREDIENTS TO AVOID			
Almonds	Heartnuts	Nut oils
Anacardium nuts	Hickory nuts	Nut paste
Artificial nuts	Indian nuts (pine nuts)	Nut pieces
Beechnuts	Japanese walnuts	Nutella spread
Brazil nuts	Lychee nuts (lichee, litchi)	Pecans
Bush nuts	Macadamia nuts	Pesto
Butternuts	Marzipan	Pili nuts
Cashews	Mashuga nuts	Pine nuts (pignoli, pigñolia, pignons, pinions, piñons, Indian nuts)
Chestnuts	Nangai nuts	
Chinquapins	Nougat	
Coconuts (see Important Information below)	Nu-Nuts	
	Nut butters	Pistachios
Filberts	Nut extracts, natural	Pralines
Gianduia chocolate	Nut meal	Shea nuts
Ginkgo nuts	Nut meats	Walnuts
Hazelnuts	Nut milks	

MAY CONTAIN TREE NUTS

Artificial and natural flavorings

Baked goods (cookies, cakes, pastries, breads, etc.)

Baking mixes (pancake, biscuit, cookie, cake, etc.)

Barbecue sauce	Granola bars	Nut distillates/ alcoholic extract
Black walnut hull extract	Ice cream, frozen desserts	Nut extracts, artificial
Breading	Ice cream toppings	Pie crusts
Cereals	Meat-free burgers	Salads
Crackers	Mortadella luncheon meat (may contain pistachios)	Salad dressings
Crumb/streusel toppings		Trail mixes

IMPORTANT INFORMATION

* Although the coconut is considered a tree nut by the FDA, it is actually a seed—and coconut allergies are very rare. Most people with tree nut allergies are able to eat coconut without having an adverse reaction. *Always check with your child's doctor first.*

* Unlike chestnuts, which are considered tree nuts, water chestnuts come from a plant root and are safe to eat.

* Although nutmeg sounds like a nut, it is the fragrant seed of a tropical tree and safe for those with nut allergies.

Milk (Cow's)

FOODS/ INGREDIENTS TO AVOID	Milk, all forms (dry, condensed, evaporated, low-fat, nonfat, skim, solids)		
	Acidophilus milk	Half-and-Half	Milk protein hydrolysate
	Butter	Hydrolysates	Nisin preparation
	Butter acid	Ice cream	Nougat
	Butter fat	Ice milk	Pudding
	Butter esters	Lactaid	Quark
	Buttermilk	Lactalbumin	Recaldent
	Casein/caseinates (all forms)	Lactalbumin phosphate	Rennet
	Cheese	Lactate solids	Sherbet
	Cottage cheese	Lactitol monohydrate	Simplesse
	Cream		Sour cream
	Cream sauces	Lactoferrin	Sour milk solids
	Cream soups	Lactoglobulin	Tagatose
	Curds	Lactose	Whey
	Custard	Lactulose	Whey protein hydrolysate
	Dairy product solids	Lactyc yeast	
	Diacetyl	Margarine (except pareve)	Whipped cream
	Galactose		Yogurt
	Ghee	Milk fat	

MAY CONTAIN MILK	Artificial and natural flavorings		
	Baked goods (cookies, cakes, pastries, breads, etc.)		
	Baking mixes (pancake, biscuit, cookie, cake, etc.)		
	Butter flavor, artificial	Lactic acid	Nisin
	Caramel candy	Lactic acid starter culture	Nondairy products
	Caramel flavoring	Luncheon meats, hot dogs, sausage	Nougat
	Chocolate		Rice cheese
	High protein flour	Margarine	Soy cheese

IMPORTANT INFORMATION	* Most people who are allergic to cow's milk, also experience reactions from goat's milk and sheep's milk.

Eggs

FOODS/ INGREDIENTS TO AVOID	Anything with the word "egg" (nog, roll, etc.)	

Albumin (albumen)	Hollandaise sauce	Ovotransferrin
Apovitellin	Livetin	Ovovitelia
Dried egg	Lysozyme	Ovovitellin
Egg substitutes (unless vegan)	Mayonnaise	Powdered egg
Egg solids	Meringue	Silici albuminate
Egg whites	Meringue powder	Simplesse
Eggnog	Ovalbumin	Surimi (imitation crabmeat)
Fat substitutes	Ovoglobulin	Vitellin
Globulin	Ovomucin	
	Ovomucoid	

MAY CONTAIN EGG	Artificial and natural flavorings	

Most baked goods (cookies, cakes, pastries, etc.)

Most custards, puddings

Lecithin	Noodles	Pasta
Marzipan	Nougat	

IMPORTANT INFORMATION

* Eggs from ducks, turkeys, geese, quail, etc. are characteristically cross-reactive with chicken eggs, and should be avoided.

* Be aware that egg wash is often used to add shine to pretzels, breads, rolls, and other baked goods.

* Eggs and egg derivatives may be contained in the foamy toppings of cappuccinos and other specialty coffees.

Wheat

**FOODS/
INGREDIENTS
TO AVOID**

Flour (all-purpose, bread, cake, durum, enriched, pastry, self-rising, stone-ground, steel-ground, whole wheat)

Wheat (berries, bran, germ, gluten, malt, starch, sprouts)

Beer	Fu	Semolina
Bran	Germ	Shoyu soy sauce
Bulgur (bulghur)	Gluten	Spelt
Bread crumbs	Hydrolyzed wheat protein	Sprouted wheat
Cereal extract		Tabbouleh
Club wheat	Kamut	Triticale
Couscous	Malt, malt extract	Triticum
Cracker meal	Matzoh (matza, matzah, matzo, matsoh)	Triticosecale
Crackers		Vital wheat gluten
Durum	Matzoh meal	Wheat bran hydrolysate
Einkorn	Noodles	Wheat germ oil
Emmer	Pasta	Wheatgrass
Farina	Seitan	Wheat protein isolate

**MAY CONTAIN
WHEAT**

Artificial and natural flavorings

Most baked goods (bread, cookies, crackers, etc.)

Most baking mixes; cereals; pie crusts (pancake, biscuit, cookie, cake, etc.)

Caramel color	Monosodium glutamate (MSG)	Tamari soy sauce (see Important Information below)
Dextrin		
Food starch (gelatinized, modified, vegetable)	Oats (see Important Information below)	Teriyaki sauce
Glucose syrup	Soy sauce	Textured vegetable protein
Hydrolyzed vegetable protein	Surimi (imitation crabmeat)	Vegetable gum
Maltodextrin		

**IMPORTANT
INFORMATION**

* Oats and oat flour are often processed in facilities that also handle wheat (and other gluten-containing grains like rye and barley), so cross-contamination may occur. Be sure to purchase varieties that are labeled wheat- or gluten-free.

* Tamari is traditionally a Japanese wheat-free soy sauce. Be aware, however, that tamari varieties made with wheat are now available, so read labels carefully.

Soy

FOODS / INGREDIENTS TO AVOID	Anything with the word "soy" (beans, oil, sauce, etc.)		
	Bean curd	Nimame	Supro
	Bean skin	Okara	Tamari soy sauce
	Edamame	Olean	Tempeh
	Hydrolyzed soy protein	Shoyu soy sauce	Teriyaki sauce
	Imitation bacon bits	Soy isoflavones	Textured vegetable protein
	Kinako flour	Soy protein concentrate	Tofu
	Kouridofu	Soy protein isolate	Tofutti
	Kyodofu	Soya, soya flour	Yakidofu
	Lecithin	Soybean curd	Yuba
	Miso	Soybean granules	
	Natto	Soybean paste	

MAY CONTAIN SOY	Artificial and natural flavorings	
	Asian dishes	
	Manufactured food products (see Important Information below)	
	Bouillon (liquid, cubes, powder)	Vegetable broth
		Vegetable gum
	Hydrolyzed plant or vegetable protein	Vegetable starch

IMPORTANT INFORMATION	* Soy is found in most manufactured food products. It is commonly used as an inexpensive filler, an emulsifier, and as a binding agent for "natural flavors."
	*Although purified soy oil and vegetable oil are supposed to be safe, be very careful. Numerous adverse reactions (some severe) have been reported after their use.

Shellfish

FOODS/ INGREDIENTS TO AVOID	**Crustaceans** *Considered major allergens*		
	Barnacles	Lobster (langouste,	Prawns
	Crab	langoustine,	Shrimp (crevette,
	Crayfish (crawdad,	Moreton,	scampi)
	crawfish, ecrevisse)	bay bugs,	
	Krill	scampi,	
		tomalley)	

Mollusks *Not considered major allergens (see Important Information below)*

Abalone	Cockles	Periwinkle
Clams	Cuttlefish	Scallops
(cherrystone,	Limpet (lapas,	Sea cucumber
geoduck,	opihi)	Sea urchin
littleneck, top	Mussels	Snails (escargot)
neck, steamers,	Octopus	Squid (calamari)
mahoganies,	Oysters	Whelk
pismo, quahog)		

MAY CONTAIN SHELLFISH	Bouillabaisse	Glucosamine	Sashimi
	Chowder	seafood flavoring	Surimi
	Cuttlefish ink	(e.g. crab or	Sushi
	Fish stock	clam extract)	

IMPORTANT INFORMATION

* Shellfish fall into two categories—crustaceans and mollusks. Only crustaceans are considered major food allergens. For this reason, FALCPA does not require mollusks to be listed on ingredient labels. *Your child's doctor, however, may advise avoiding mollusks.*

Fish

FOODS / INGREDIENTS TO AVOID	Any vertebrate fish with fins (salmon, tuna, cod, bass swordfish, etc.)		
	Caviar (fish eggs)	Sashimi	Sushi
	Fish gelatin	Surimi (imitation crabmeat)	Worcestershire sauce (contains anchovies)
	Roe (fish eggs)		
MAY CONTAIN FISH	Caesar salad (some contain anchovies)		
	Caesar salad dressing		
IMPORTANT INFORMATION	* Some individuals with a fish allergy may be able to tolerate fish oil supplements. *Always check with the doctor first.*		

BENEFITS OF HEALTHFUL ALLERGEN-FREE SNACKING

Let's face it, it's hard enough to find healthy snacks in most grocery stores, and it's even more of a challenge to find ones that are allergen-free. Commercially made crackers, chips, trail mixes, energy bars, cookies, and other baked goods are often highly processed and loaded with sugar, salt, trans fats, preservatives, food colorings, and other undesirable ingredients. This is why the recipes in this book focus not only on allergen-free snacks that kids will love, but also on choices that are healthy and nutritious.

Making your own snacks puts you in control of using safe ingredients that your child can eat without worrying about an allergic reaction. And the recipes in this book are designed to help. In addition to being allergen free, the snacks we share with you are also free of gluten and refined white sugar. As an added bonus, they are also wholesome, natural, and nutritious—not to mention satisfying and delicious.

Snack foods are often high in calories and short on nutrition, but the plant-based choices in this book are characteristically high in whole grains, rich in fiber, and low in calories. You'll see how easy it is to prepare impressive and tantalizing snacks that will fill your kids up in a healthy way.

The benefits your child will gain from healthful snacking cannot be denied. Encouraging the development of good eating/snacking habits will help your child maintain a healthy weight, experience increased energy, and have a lowered chance of getting sick. Furthermore, good habits that begin at a young age are likely to carry through to adulthood.

Encourages Good Eating Habits

Are you familiar with the term "mindless eating"? If you've ever found yourself munching away while sitting in front of the TV or a computer screen without even realizing that you're eating, let alone *how much* you are eating; if your hand has a tendency to keep plunging into that snack bowl and then make its way to your mouth with no thought involved, then you have experienced mindless eating firsthand.

Unfortunately, we have become a nation of mindless eaters who snack out of boredom, to be social, or simply because the food is in front of us. These poor eating habits coupled with lack of exercise and unhealthy food choices play an undeniable role in the country's growing obesity problem, which currently affects nearly 30 percent of adults over age twenty, and around 17 percent of children and adolescents between the ages of two and nineteen.

Helping children develop good eating/snacking habits (nutrient-dense, low-calorie foods that are eaten sensibly and in proper portions) will encourage them to become "mindful" eaters. Instead of eating simply for the sake of eating, your child will always be aware of when, what, and how much he or she is eating. A beneficial habit that will last a lifetime.

Increases Energy

Because the snacks in this book are filled with fiber-rich complex carbohydrates—whole grains, fruits, and vegetables—they provide fuel for the body. Complex carbohydrates, which are digested slowly, will help your child feel satisfied for long periods after eating. They also help stabilize blood sugar and maintain even energy levels. We call them "upper foods."

On the other hand, we avoid simple carbohydrates, such as white sugar, white flour, and any products that contain them. These refined, processed "downer foods," contain no or very little fiber, which means they are digested quickly. This causes blood sugar levels to spike quickly and then drop dramatically—in other words the body initially feels a quick burst of energy that is soon followed by a noticeable energy drop. Simple carbs are also linked to cravings, compulsive eating, and irritability.

So you can feel good about fueling your child with our fiber-filled snacks. They will help curb those hunger pangs and provide the needed energy to get through any slumps during the day.

Promotes Good Health

Along with being fiber-rich, our kid-friendly snacks are packed with vitamins and minerals for increased nutritional value. And as an added bonus, they don't contain any artery-clogging saturated fats.

Saturated fats contribute to high levels of *low-density lipoproteins* (LDLs) or bad cholesterol, a leading risk factor in coronary heart disease, diabetes, and stroke. A recent issue of *Annals of Internal Medicine* published the results of a study that examined the link between bad cholesterol levels in young adults and the development of heart disease later on. Under the guidance of Dr. Mark J. Pletcher, researchers at the University of California, San Francisco, analyzed data from 3,528 men and women who had been tracked for twenty years by the CARDIA study (Coronary Artery Risk Development in Young Adults). At the beginning of the study, the age of the participants ranged from eighteen to thirty years old. The researchers found that the participants with histories of high LDL levels as young adults were five and a half times more likely to have a buildup of calcium in their coronary arteries than those with low LDL levels.

The fats used in our recipes come from heart-healthy foods like avocados and oils such as olive, sunflower, and grapeseed. These fats help raise the *high-density lipoproteins* (HDLs), also known as good cholesterol. HDLs help rid the body of LDLs and reduce the risk of heart disease and stroke. A growing amount of evi-

DOGGONE FOODS!

Did you know that even our furry friends can be allergic to certain foods? Soy, wheat gluten, dairy, fish, beef, and lamb are among the biggest offenders for both cats and dogs—and itchy skin rashes are the usual symptoms. Interestingly, these foods are also the most common products found in commercial pet foods. The good news is that hypoallergenic food is available.

In addition to foods that cause allergies, a number of foods can actually be toxic to animals like cats and dogs and make them seriously ill. Never give the following to your furry friends:

❑ **AVOCADO.** The skin, fruit, and pit of avocados are toxic and can cause gastrointestinal and respiratory problems.

❑ **CHOCOLATE.** Chocolate contains a stimulant that can affect heart rate and the central nervous system.

❑ **FRUIT PITS/SEEDS.** The pits and seeds of many fruits, such as apples, pears, peaches, and cherries, contain poisonous cyanide. When ingested, serious respiratory problems or even death can result; they can also become lodged in the intestinal tract.

❑ **GRAPES, RAISINS, CURRANTS.** These fruits contain a toxin that can cause kidney damage.

❑ **MACADAMIA NUTS/WALNUTS.** Nuts in general are not good for pets; but these two varieties can affect the heart, muscles, and the nervous and digestive systems.

❑ **MILK/DAIRY PRODUCTS.** Dairy products contain lactose, which may cause diarrhea and other digestive issues.

❑ **ONIONS/GARLIC.** Both onions and garlic contain sulfoxides and disulfides, which can damage red blood cells and cause anemia, especially in cats.

❑ **SALT.** Sodium can lead to a number of serious problems including kidney failure and neurological conditions like seizures and coma.

❑ **XYLITOL.** This sweetener, found in many sugar-free candies, chewing gums, breath mints, and baked goods can cause liver failure.

❑ **YEAST DOUGH.** When it is ingested, yeast dough can expand in the digestive system and cause pain, bloating, and a possible rupture.

dence also shows that HDLs may even offer extra protection against certain cancers.

SUMMING IT UP

As mentioned earlier, the only way to prevent your child from having an allergic food reaction is simply to avoid the problem food. But avoidance doesn't mean your child has to feel deprived. It doesn't mean a limited diet of bland, unappealing meals and snacks.

As you will see, when it comes to those lunchbox goodies, after-school snacks, and party treats, your child is going to look forward to all of the delicious choices that are found in this book. And it doesn't matter which of the top allergenic foods affect your child or if the allergy is mild or severe—he or she can enjoy all of the snacks in this book without fear of a reaction. Low in fat and calories, yet high in flavor, these snacks are not just for kids with allergies. Everyone can enjoy them!

2

Stocking the Kitchen

If you have children or other family members with food allergies, it's a good idea to keep a variety of kitchen staples on hand. Having the right ingredients will allow you to prepare healthy, allergen-free meals and snacks, including the recipes in this book, at any time.

In the last chapter, we talked about the foods and ingredients *to avoid*. This chapter is all about the best ones *to choose*. One of our strongest recommendations is to select foods that are as close to their natural state as possible. This means whole foods, including fresh fruits and vegetables, whole grains, and beans that preferably are locally grown. It also means using unrefined natural sweeteners like honey, fruit juice, date sugar, and maple syrup. Whole foods and whole food products are unprocessed (or minimally processed) so they are close to their natural, nutrient-packed state. And organically grown foods and the products made from them are the best.

WHY ORGANIC?

Organic foods are grown in rich soil that is free of pesticides and synthetic fertilizers. They do not contain chemical additives, hormones, or preservatives. And since they are very close to their natural state, they taste better, too.

Another important reason to choose organic —especially for those with allergies—is that it means avoiding *genetically modified food* (GM food), which comes from *genetically modified organisms* (GMOs). Simply put, the genes of GM plants have been altered or artificially manipulated to mix and match the DNA of totally different species, often for the purpose of growing a bigger, better version of the crop or to create one that is resistant to pesticides and herbicides. The genetically modified Flavr Savr Tomato, for example, was spliced with a gene that prevented the breakdown of its cell walls, resulting in a firmer tomato with a longer shelf life.

Nearly 80 percent of the corn and over 90 percent of the soybeans grown in the United States are genetically modified. The most popular herbicide-resistant GM crops are the Monsanto Company's Roundup Ready crops, which are engineered to be resistant to Monsanto's own broad-spectrum herbicide called Roundup. Because the plants are resistant to the herbicide, growers are able to douse their fields with it, killing the weeds and pests without harming the crops themselves. Growers no longer need to till the soil to control weeds.

While there have been many arguments in favor of genetically modified foods, there are a growing number of reasons against them. Concerns for the environment and human health are the most obvious. And those with allergies need to be especially concerned. One of the biggest fears is that splicing genes between two different species can inadvertently incorporate an allergenic protein into the modified crop or cause the formation of a new one. Cross-pollination is another concern. A growing number of researchers are finding links between the consumption of GM crops and the creation or worsening of food allergies.

Organic foods do not contain genetically modified ingredients, so it is best to choose them whenever possible. This is especially recommended when buying soybeans and corn (the most common GM crops) and any products that contain them.

"9 IS FINE"

Another way to avoid genetically modified produce is by checking the Price Look-Up (PLU) code, which is found on a tiny label that is stuck on the fruit or vegetable. The PLU code for GM produce has five numbers that begin with the number 8. Organically grown fruits and vegetables have five numbers that begin with the number 9. The PLU code for non-GM produce that is grown through conventional farming methods (which likely means the use of pesticides, herbicides, and/or chemical fertilizers) has only four numbers. An easy way to remember organic varieties is by keeping in mind that "9 is fine."

WHERE TO SHOP

Fortunately, due to an increasing demand for whole and organic foods, when it comes to shopping, you have a number of good options.

Farmers' markets that sell fresh organic produce are located in towns and cities throughout the United States. Buying from local farmers means getting freshly picked fruits and vegetables—and the fresher the produce, the greater its nutritional value. As soon as that apple is picked, its vitamin and mineral content begins to diminish. Most of the produce found on supermarket shelves was picked four to seven days earlier and transported an average of 1,500 miles. Local farmers' markets assure fresher foods than what you'll find in the supermarket, and you will be supporting local growers. To locate a farmer's market in your area, visit the following website for a national map of market locations: *www.ams.usda.gov/farmersmarkets/map.htm*.

Natural foods markets also sell whole foods like fruits, vegetables, whole grains, and whole grain products that are typically organic. Many of the larger stores offer extensive selections, and their product turnover rate is usually quick, which is a good indication of freshness. Although natural foods markets are more expensive than most other stores, they tend to support local farmers and sustainable agriculture practices.

A growing number of supermarkets are beginning to carry whole foods and organic products. They are conveniently located, which is a plus; however, their selection is often limited and product turnover may be slow, which means compromised freshness.

Finally, you can also purchase organic foods online. We have bought a number of grains and grain products from reputable online companies, and have included a list of these responsible suppliers in the Resources beginning on page 123.

Another thing to keep in mind when buying organic is that packaged foods often contain multiple ingredients. The word "organic" appearing on a label does not necessarily mean that the product is 100-percent organic. (See the inset on "Organic Product Labeling" below.)

ALLERGEN-FREE KITCHEN MUST-HAVES

The list of allergen-free foods and ingredients beginning on the next page is certainly not complete, but it does include the products we recommend to keep handy in your kitchen. (Many are used in our snack recipes.) The products you choose will depend, of course, on the particular type of food allergy your child has. When buying packaged items, always check ingredient labels carefully, even those products you have bought before—manufacturers often change product ingredients without warning. A list of recommended product brands and companies that sell allergen-free foods is found in the Resources, beginning on page 123.

ORGANIC PRODUCT LABELING

Understanding organic labeling can be a little confusing, especially for products that contain more than one ingredient. In an effort to help consumers understand the organic content of the food they buy, the USDA has established the following labeling rules:

SINGLE-INGREDIENT FOODS

For fruits, vegetables, and other single-ingredient foods, a sticker version of the USDA Organic seal (above) may appear on the products themselves or on a sign above them.

MULTI-INGREDIENT FOODS

For packaged foods that contain more than one ingredient, the following labeling terms are used to indicate their organic content:

■ **100% ORGANIC.** The product must contain 100% organic ingredients. It is permitted to use the USDA seal.

■ **ORGANIC.** The product must contain 95 to 100% organic ingredients. It is permitted to use the USDA seal.

■ **MADE WITH ORGANIC INGREDIENTS.** The product must contain at least 70% organic ingredients.

■ **CONTAINS ORGANIC INGREDIENTS.** The product contains less than 70% organic ingredients.

It is also important to know that even if a producer is certified organic, using the USDA Organic seal is voluntary. In addition, the process of becoming certified is very demanding, and not all producers of organic foods are willing to go through it, especially small farming operations. For this reason, never hesitate to ask vendors, such as those at farmers' markets, how their products are grown.

Milk Substitutes

Rice milk, oat milk and hemp milk. For optimal nutrition, choose organic varieties that are fortified with calcium, vitamins D, B and E. Coconut milk is another milk substitute.

Egg Substitutes

Ener-G Egg Replacer (for baking only). To make your own egg-free substitute for baking purposes, try any of the following ingredient combinations, each of which is equivalent to one egg:

■ 1 tablespoon flaxseed meal plus 3 tablespoons warm water. Let sit three minutes.

■ 1 teaspoon baking powder plus 1 tablespoon apple cider vinegar.

■ 1 tablespoon agar plus 1 tablespoon water.

Oils

Grapeseed, safflower, sunflower, sesame, extra-virgin olive oil.

Baking Products and Thickeners

Baking powder (aluminum and albumin-free), baking soda, arrowroot, tapioca flour, agar powder, potato starch.

Seeds and Seed Butters

Flaxseeds, flaxseed meal, pumpkin seeds, sesame seeds, sunflower seeds, sunflower butter, tahini (sesame seed butter). Please note that if your child is allergic to tree nuts, all of these seeds (with the exception of sesame seeds) are rarely allergenic and considered acceptable. Be aware, however, that although sesame seeds are not on the current list of top allergens by the FDA, reactions to them—often serious—are on the rise.

Breads and Bread Products

Gluten-free/allergen-free varieties of bread and bread crumbs, bagels, buns, muffins, pitas, rolls; brown rice tortillas, corn tortillas.

Cereals (dry, ready-to-eat)

Gluten-free/allergen-free varieties, such as amaranth flakes, corn flakes, flax flakes, oat circles, puffed millet, puffed rice.

Fresh Fruits (preferably organic)

Apples, peaches, pears, bananas, etc., and citrus fruits (lemons, oranges, grapefruits, tangerines, mandarins, clementines).

Fresh Vegetables (preferably organic)

Vegetables, such as avocados, broccoli, cabbage, carrots, cauliflower, corn (organic only), cucumbers, eggplant, garlic, lettuce, mushrooms, onions, peas, potatoes, scallions, spinach, squash, sweet potatoes (or yams), tomatoes.

Sweeteners (preferably organic)

Agave nectar, date sugar, fruit juice (orange, apple), fruit concentrate (frozen), fruit syrup, honey, pure maple syrup, rice syrup.

Canned and Bottled Goods

Beans (black beans, chickpeas, kidney beans, etc.), corn (organic only), fruit-sweetened jams, olives, pumpkin purée, tomato sauce.

Snack Foods and Frozen Desserts

Raisins and other dried fruit (unsulfured); gluten-free/allergen-free products like flax crackers, oat crackers, popcorn, rice cakes, and rice crackers; and frozen items such as frozen fruit, sorbets, and Rice Dream brand frozen treats.

Pasta and Noodles

Brown rice pasta, corn pasta, quinoa pasta, Papadini lentil/bean pasta, rice noodles (rice sticks).

Seasonings and Flavor Enhancers

Apple cider vinegar, balsamic vinegar, black pepper, carob powder, cinnamon, fresh/dried herbs (basil, rosemary, thyme, cilantro, oregano), garlic powder, garlic salt, ketchup, lemons, limes, mustard, nutmeg, pickles, salsa, sea salt, Tabasco or other hot sauce, vanilla extract (wheat-free).

Grains and Flours

Amaranth flour, brown rice, brown rice flour, buckwheat flour, chickpeas (garbanzo beans), chickpea flour, cornmeal, millet, oats, oat flour, potato flour, quinoa, quinoa flour, and/or teff flour.

FACTS ON FATS

FRIEND FATS

According to the American Heart Association, a heart-healthy diet can contain up to 30 percent of calories from fat, provided that most of the fat is unsaturated. Unsaturated fats, which include monounsaturated and polyunsaturated varieties, are "friendly fats" that lower harmful LDL cholesterol levels. Monounsaturated fats are found in olive oil and canola oil. Polyunsaturated fats are found in corn, flax, grapeseed, safflower, sesame, and sunflower oils.

FOE FATS

Saturated fats are not your friends! They increase LDL cholesterol (the bad cholesterol), which clogs arteries and can lead to heart disease. Saturated fat, found mainly in animal sources like whole milk, butter, and fatty meats, has also been linked to an increased risk of type-2 diabetes.

Another "foe" to avoid is hydrogenated fat. This type of fat is created when hydrogen is added to an oil (often unsaturated) to make it solid at room temperature. During this process, the fat becomes more saturated. Trans fats, considered the worst of the saturated fats, are cre-ated during the processing of foods through partial hydrogenation. Trans fats are often found in commercial products such as crackers, snack chips, baked goods, and frozen items like waffles and French fries.

RECIPE CHOICES

We use "heart healthy" fats in our snack recipes, such as those found in cold-pressed virgin and extra-virgin olive oils and grapeseed oil (organic, of course). The beneficial essential fatty acids they contain are also critical for nerve and brain functioning. Unfortunately, many commercial varieties of these oils are subjected to chemical and heat processing that causes the formation of harmful free radicals. This is why we advocate using organic, cold-pressed, minimally processed oils. We also recommend storing the oil in a dark glass container and keeping it in the refrigerator to prevent rancidity.

As for using other oils, we avoid nut oils—for obvious reasons—and do not advocate the use of corn oil, which, unless it is organic, is likely to contain GMOs. We also avoid canola oil because of the controversy regarding its safety.

Be aware that oats and oat flour are often processed in facilities that also handle wheat (and other gluten-containing grains like rye and barley), so cross-contamination may occur. Make sure to purchase varieties that are certified wheat- or gluten-free.

Once again, all of the foods and products listed above are safe for those who are allergic to any of the top eight food allergens—peanuts, tree nuts, milk, eggs, wheat, soy, fish, and crustacean shellfish. They are also gluten-free, making them acceptable choices for those with celiac disease. It isn't necessary to stock all of the recommended ingredients, as your choices will depend on the foods your child has to avoid.

RECIPE ADJUSTING

When you have a child or any family member with food allergies, you will undoubtedly find yourself on a constant search for "safe" foods and recipes that are allergen-free. The good news is

that due to the growing number of people with food allergies, there is also a growing number of available recipes and meal ideas. Whether it is through books, magazines, or Internet sites, you can find plenty of recipes that cater either to one specific food allergen or many.

Although it is helpful (and certainly convenient) that so many allergy-specific recipes exist, it can be just as helpful to know how to adapt those recipes that are not allergen-free. By knowing how to replace allergenic ingredients with safe substitutions, you can make new (and often improved) versions of those family favorite holiday cookies or that delicious-sounding muffin recipe you came across in a magazine. Knowing how to adapt and adjust is a skill that often takes just a little guidance, patience, and experience. To help you out, we have created the chart "Ingredient Substitutions for Recipe Adjustments" on pages 28 and 29. In it we have listed some of the most common allergenic ingredients found in recipes along with some suggested ingredient substitutions.

Fruit and Veggie Wash

Always wash your fruits and vegetables before eating. Even organic varieties are likely to contain bacteria from processing, shipping, and handling. Here's the simple recipe we use and recommend:

1. Place the ingredients in a spray bottle and shake well.

2. Spray the fruit/veggies with the wash, scrub gently with your hands, then rinse with cold water.

3. Store any remaining wash in the refrigerator.

1 cup water

2 tablespoons fresh lemon juice, vinegar, salt, or baking soda

SOME HELPFUL TIPS

Before you start preparing the fantastic kid-friendly snacks in the following chapters, we wanted to share a few quick tips and guidelines with you. Hopefully, you will find them helpful when making these tasty treats.

❏ In most recipes, honey is our liquid sweetener of choice; however, feel free to use equal amounts of maple syrup, agave nectar, rice syrup, or another natural liquid sweetener instead.

❏ Honey can sometimes crystallize. If this happens, place it in a heat-resistant glass cup or container and set it in a pan or bowl of hot water. As it begins to heat up, stir the honey until it returns to a smooth liquid state.

❏ If a recipe calls for oil and a liquid sweetener, first measure the oil. After emptying out the oil, use the same measuring cup (don't clean it) to measure the sweetener. The oil residue on the cup will allow the sticky sweetener to slide out easily.

❏ For even baking, unless otherwise instructed in a recipe, bake the food on the center oven rack.

❏ To get the most juice out of fresh lemons, limes, or oranges, roll them against the kitchen countertop before squeezing.

❏ When using oat flour, make sure it is certified pure oat flour with no possible presence of wheat or gluten.

❏ We use nondairy rice and oat milks in our recipes. If your child is not allergic to soy or tree nuts, you can use soy and/or almond milk instead.

❏ For the sake of time, we use canned beans in our recipes. We recommend organic varieties that are free of salt.

HERBS FRESH OR DRIED?

When it comes to using herbs and spices, we recommend fresh when possible. If using dried, be sure to check expiration dates. Most dried herbs lose their potency within a few months.

1 tablespoon fresh = 1 teaspoon dried

❏ Our recipes generally call for oat flour and brown rice flour; however, amaranth, buckwheat, chickpea (garbanzo), millet, potato, quinoa, and teff flours can be substituted in equal amounts.

Many of the snacks in this book can be made in advance and stored in the refrigerator or freezer. Having a few of your child's favorite treats on hand will allow you to quickly satisfy any snack attacks with safe and healthy choices.

HAPPY SNACKING!

Everybody loves to snack, especially kids! Now that you're armed with the information you'll need to prepare healthful, allergen-free snacks, it's time to get started. Remember, just because your child has dietary restrictions, he or she can still enjoy snacks that are absolutely yummy, satisfying, and even fun to eat! Deprivation should never be an option! And making your child's meals and snacks yourself will allow you to monitor the ingredients to guarantee their safety . . . and give you peace of mind. So let's go. It's time for some happy snacking!

Ingredient Substitutions for Recipe Adjustments

When you are adjusting the ingredients in a recipe to suit the particular needs of your child, you may find the following substitution chart helpful. It offers some suggested ingredient options for a number of common food allergens. Be aware that these substitutions do not include any of the eight major food allergens. Also be aware that, depending on your child's specific allergy, you can expand these options. For instance, if your child is allergic to dairy but not soy, you can add soymilk as a milk option.

ALLERGENIC FOOD	SUGGESTED SUBSTITUTIONS	BEST USES
Cocoa	Carob powder in equal measure.	As a flavor-enhancer in smoothies and other beverages, desserts, and baked goods.
Cow's milk	Rice milk, hemp milk, oat milk in equal measure.	As an ingredient in baked goods, smoothies, and light cream-style soups and sauces.
Buttermilk	Mix 1 tablespoon lemon juice or apple cider vinegar with 1 cup of the milks listed above. Let sit a few minutes to thicken.	As an ingredient in baked goods and cream-style sauces.
Cream	Potato purée in equal measure.	As a thickener in soups and sauces.
Egg (1 large)	Mix 1 tablespoon flaxseed meal with 3 tablespoons water. Let sit a few minutes to thicken.	As a binder in baked goods.
	$1/4$ cup applesauce or puréed fruit.*	As a binder in baked goods. Also adds moisture.

ALLERGENIC FOOD	SUGGESTED SUBSTITUTIONS	BEST USES
Egg (1 large)	Mix 1 tablespoon agar powder with 1 tablespoon water.	As a binder in baked goods.
	Mix 2 teaspoons baking powder with 2 tablespoons water and 1 tablespoon vegetable oil.	As a leavening agent in baked goods.
	Ener-G Egg Replacer (prepare as directed on package).	As a leavening agent in baked goods.
Peanut butter / Nut butters	Sunflower seed butter and sesame seed butter (tahini) in equal measure.	As an ingredient in baked goods, desserts, and smoothies.
Wheat flour (1 cup)**	$3/4$ cup brown rice flour, $3/4$ cup potato flour, $3/4$ cup chickpea flour, 1 cup tapioca flour, or 1 $1/4$ cups oat flour *Suggested Flour Combination:* $2/3$ cup rice flour + $1/4$ cup potato flour + 2 tablespoons tapioca flour	As an ingredient in baked goods, and as a thickener in soups and sauces.
White sugar (1 cup)†	$3/4$ cup agave nectar $3/4$ cup date sugar $3/4$ cup honey $3/4$ cup maple syrup $3/4$ cup rice syrup	As an ingredient in baked goods, desserts, and smoothies.

* When using puréed fruit, baked goods tend to come out a little heavy and dense. For this reason, adding an additional $1/2$ teaspoon baking powder to the recipe is recommended.

** When making flour substitutions for baked goods, don't expect to achieve the same texture and consistency as with wheat flour. For best results, experimenting may be necessary, depending on the particular recipe.

† Although white sugar is not an allergenic food, it is included in this table because it is a common ingredient in many recipes and not a healthy choice.

IMPORTANT WORD ABOUT THE RECIPES

The snacks in this book are made without eggs, cow's milk or other dairy products, soy, wheat (or other grains containing gluten), peanuts, tree nuts, fish, or shellfish—the most common allergenic foods according to the current assessment of the U.S. Food and Drug Administration.

Of course, most people with food allergies are allergic to one, maybe even a few of these ingredients—but not to all of them. For this reason, keep in mind that you can prepare the recipes in this book as written or alter the ingredients to suit your child's individual dietary needs. For instance, if nut allergies are not a problem, feel free to add some chopped walnuts to a cookie recipe, add peanut butter to the Carob Fudge Brownies, or use almond butter as a spread. If your child isn't allergic to dairy, top his or her pizza with some shredded mozzarella or a sprinkling of Parmesan. You get the idea.

Your child may also be allergic to an ingredient in a recipe that is not considered one of the major food allergens—ingredients such as tomatoes, onions, peaches, and sesame seeds to name a few. You can either prepare the recipe without the ingredient or try using a substitute. Simply put, you can prepare the delicious snack recipes in this book to enjoy as they are or use them as springboards for kid-pleasing variations.

Most important, no matter what you choose to do, no matter how you decide to alter the recipes, you can feel good in knowing that they are not only allergen-free, but healthy as well.

Have fun and enjoy!

3

Salsas, Dips, and Chips

Whether it's fresh salsa and tortilla chips, yummy hummus with pita crisps, or rice crackers topped with creamy bean spread, one thing is certain—crunchy chips paired with flavorful dips are welcomed snacks for kids of all ages. In this chapter, you will find some of our most delicious and nutritious kid-pleasing favorites—a delectable assortment of allergen-free salsas, dips, chutneys, and spreads, along with a variety of crisps and crackers and "things that go crunch." (And who doesn't love crunch?)

Among this chapter's tasty treats, we've included appetizing classics like Holy Guacamole!, Mummy's Yummy Hummus, and No-Egg Eggplant Dip (our version of Middle Eastern baba ghanoush). There are fruit-sweetened choices like Tangy Mango Salsa, as well as savory selections like Fun Freckled Sun Dip. We've even featured two recipes for creamy mayonnaise that are dairy- and egg-free.

Although a growing number of commercial allergen-free chips and crackers are now available, if you prefer to make your own, you'll find a nice assortment here. There are recipes for crispy Chickpea Crackers, light and flaky Oat Crisps, and Mini Crunch Cups, which you can fill with your child's favorite sweet or savory filling. We even show you how to turn nutrient-rich kale leaves into crisp snack chips.

As an added perk, the recipes are very versatile. You can, for instance, drizzle the dips over baked potatoes, add the salsas and chutneys to salads, or roll up the spreads in rice tortillas to make snackin' good sandwiches. And don't forget about adding your own creative twists to the recipes or making ingredient adjustments to satisfy your child's individual tastes and needs.

So pick a dip, select a spread, or choose a chutney. No matter which recipe you select, no matter how you serve it to your kids, they're gonna love it!

Apple-Plum Chutney

*Spoon some of this flavorful chutney onto crisp
endive leaves for a refreshing snack.
Or roll it up in the soft leaves of butter lettuce or
on a rice tortilla for a neatly packaged treat.*

Yield: About 4 cups

• • • • • • •

1 $\frac{1}{4}$ cups brown rice
vinegar

1 $\frac{3}{4}$ cups date sugar

4 cups peeled and
coarsely chopped
Granny Smith apples

1 tablespoon ground
cinnamon

1 tablespoon minced fresh
ginger, or 1 teaspoon
ground dried

1 pound firm dark
purple plums, seeded and
cut into $\frac{1}{2}$-inch pieces

$\frac{3}{4}$ cup raisins

1. Place the vinegar and date sugar in a 4-quart pot and bring to a boil over medium-high heat. Reduce the heat to low and stir gently for 2 minutes or until the sugar dissolves.

2. Add the apples, cinnamon, and ginger to the pot. Simmer uncovered about 5 minutes or until the apples start to soften.

3. Add the plums and raisins, and continue to cook another 12 minutes or until the apples and plums have softened and the mixture has thickened. Remove from the heat and let cool.

4. Serve warm, at room temperature, or chilled. Store in the refrigerator up to seven days.

CHANGE IT UP . . .

- To add a slightly tart taste, use dried cranberries or currants instead of raisins.

- For an added spark of flavor, include 1 chopped medium onion in Step 2 above, and in any of the following variations.

- For Apple-Pear Chutney, substitute 2 cups chopped firm pears for the plums.

- To make an Apple-Cranberry version, substitute 2 cups fresh or frozen cranberries for the plums, and add 1 tablespoon orange zest.

- For an Apple-Mango version, use 2 cups cubed mango instead of plums.

- To create Apple-Apricot Chutney, substitute 2 cups cubed apricots for the plums.

Corny Relish

This is a fun party snack, especially in the middle of summer when corn is at its seasonal peak. Serve it in a bowl as is, or along with chips, crackers, or rice cakes.

Yield: About 2 cups

5 large ears corn, husked

2 celery stalks, finely diced

$1/2$ cup diced cucumber

$1/4$ cup finely chopped parsley

$1/4$ cup lemon juice

$1/4$ cup extra-virgin olive oil

I teaspoon sea salt

1. Add the corn to a large pot of water, bring to a boil, and cook for 10 minutes. Remove from the pot and allow to cool.

2. Remove the kernels with a sharp knife, and place in a medium bowl along with the remaining ingredients. Stir well.

3. Serve at room temperature or refrigerate and serve cold. Store in the refrigerator up to a week.

CHANGE IT UP . . .

- Instead of cucumber, add diced pickles (sweet, dill, any kind your kids like).

- For added flavor, add a tablespoon or two of finely chopped red onion.

Rockin' Raw Cranberry Relish

No additional sweetener is needed for this easy-to-make tasty fruit relish.

Yield: About 2 cups

I orange, peeled, seeded, and sliced

I lemon, peeled, seeded, and sliced

2 dates, pitted and chopped

2 cups fresh cranberries

1. Place the orange slices, lemon slices, and dates in a food processor and blend for a minute or until thick and pulpy.

2. Add the cranberries and continue to blend for 20 seconds or until coarsely chopped.

3. Serve immediately or refrigerate and serve chilled. Store in the refrigerator up to five days.

Festive Fiesta Salsa

Fresh corn kernels add delicious sweetness and just the right crunch to this refreshing salsa.

Yield: About 2 cups

• • • • • • • •

1 cup cooked corn kernels

1 large tomato, seeded and diced

2 scallions, finely sliced

2 tablespoons chopped fresh cilantro

$\frac{1}{4}$ cup lime juice

1 small clove garlic, minced

1 teaspoon sea salt

1. Place all of the ingredients in a medium bowl and mix well.

2. Cover and marinate in the refrigerator at least 1 hour.

3. Serve chilled. Store in the refrigerator up to a week.

CHANGE IT UP . . .

• For added color and crunch, add $\frac{1}{4}$ cup chopped bell pepper (any color).

• If your kids like a little "heat," try adding a seeded, coarsely chopped jalapeño chile.

Tangy Mango Salsa

Red wine vinegar adds just the right "tang" to this mango-sweetened salsa.

Yield: About 4 cups

• • • • • • • •

6 medium tomatoes, diced

2 celery stalks, diced

2 mangos, diced

$\frac{1}{2}$ cup chopped fresh cilantro

$\frac{1}{4}$ cup red wine vinegar

$\frac{1}{2}$ teaspoon sea salt

$\frac{1}{4}$ teaspoon ground black pepper

1. Place all of the ingredients in a large bowl and mix well.

2. Serve immediately or refrigerate and serve chilled. Store in the refrigerator up to five days.

CHANGE IT UP . . .

• For added flavor, add $\frac{1}{2}$ cup diced red onion.

Chunky Black Bean Dip

In addition to serving this delicious dip with traditional chips and crackers, try scooping a few tablespoons onto a rice tortilla and rolling it up for a tasty burrito.

1. Place the garlic, cilantro, and olive oil in a blender or food processor, and process about 20 seconds.

2. Add the beans, lime juice, and sea salt to the blender and pulse 15 to 20 seconds to form a thick, slightly chunky purée.

3. Transfer to a serving bowl and enjoy. Store in the refrigerator up to five days.

CHANGE IT UP . . .

• Use lemon juice instead of lime juice.

• Substitute chickpeas for the black beans.

• If your kids like a little "heat," try adding a seeded, coarsely chopped jalapeño chile.

Yield: About 1 cup

. . . .

1 small clove garlic, minced

$1/2$ cup loosely packed cilantro leaves

2 tablespoons extra-virgin olive oil

15-ounce can black beans, rinsed and drained

1 tablespoon lime juice, or to taste

1 teaspoon sea salt

No-Egg Eggplant Dip

Yield: About 3 cups

- 1 large eggplant
- 1 cup diced tomatoes
- $\frac{1}{2}$ cup finely chopped yellow onion
- $\frac{1}{4}$ cup finely chopped parsley
- $\frac{1}{4}$ cup red wine vinegar
- 2 tablespoons extra-virgin olive oil
- $\frac{1}{2}$ teaspoon garlic powder (optional)
- $\frac{1}{4}$ teaspoon dried oregano
- $\frac{1}{4}$ teaspoon black pepper
- $\frac{1}{4}$ teaspoon sea salt

Serve this chunky dip with gluten-free pita bread, rice crackers, or Flaky Oat Crisps (page 49).

1. Preheat the oven to 375°F.

2. Place the eggplant on a baking sheet and put in the oven. Turning occasionally, bake the eggplant for 50 to 60 minutes, or until tender when pierced with a fork. Remove and let cool.

3. Cut the cooled eggplant in half lengthwise. Scoop out the pulp into a large mixing bowl and coarsely mash with a fork. Discard the skin.

4. Add the remaining ingredients and stir well. Cover and refrigerate at least 1 hour.

5. Serve chilled. Store in the refrigerator up to five days.

Grape-ful Salsa

Yield: About 2 cups

- 1 cup red seedless grapes
- 4 medium tomatoes, coarsely chopped
- 2 celery stalks, finely diced
- 2 tablespoons fresh cilantro leaves
- 2 tablespoons lime juice
- 1 small clove garlic, minced
- 1 teaspoon sea salt
- 1 teaspoon hot sauce (optional)

Red grapes add sweetness to this flavorful salsa. Serve it on baked tortilla chips topped with slices of avocado, or cup it in a butter lettuce leaf.

1. Cut the grapes in half and place in a medium mixing bowl. Add the remaining ingredients and mix well.

2. Marinate in the refrigerator at least 30 minutes (the longer it marinates, the stronger the flavors).

3. Serve chilled. Store in the refrigerator up to five days.

Holy Guacamole!

*Packed with nutrition, creamy rich avocados are the
star ingredient in this delicious guacamole.*

1. Cut the avocados in half. Spoon the flesh into a large bowl and
mash. Reserve one of the seeds.

2. Add the tomato, scallions, lemon juice, garlic, and sea salt to
the avocado and stir well.

3. Serve immediately or refrigerate and serve chilled. If refrig-
erating, transfer the guacamole to an airtight container, place
the reserved seed in the middle, and cover. (The seed will help
prevent the mixture from turning brown.) Store in the refrigerator up to two days.

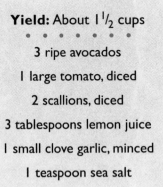

Yield: About 1 1/2 cups

• • • • • • •

3 ripe avocados

1 large tomato, diced

2 scallions, diced

3 tablespoons lemon juice

1 small clove garlic, minced

1 teaspoon sea salt

CHANGE IT UP . . .

• For sweeter flavor, use lime juice instead of lemon.

• Add 1/4 cup of salsa for added spiciness and texture.

MMMM . . . MAYONNAISE

Mayonnaise is so versatile. You can use it as a sandwich spread, as a flavorful addition to salads, or even as a creamy dipping sauce for French fries and crisp raw veggies.

When it comes to commercial mayonnaise, we recommend Follow Your Heart brand Soy-Free Vegenaise Dressing and Sandwich Spread. It's smooth, creamy, and tastes delicious. But if you would like to try making your own, here are two recipes that are made in a blender. Just be aware that both recipes require time and patience—adding the oil must be done very, very slowly in order for the mixture to emulsify properly. We recommend using a condiment squeeze bottle or an eye-dropper for this. Both recipes take anywhere from 10 to 15 minutes to add the oil. For this reason, you may want to turn off the blender every few minutes to let the motor rest. Use this time to scrape down the sides of the blender.

Dreamy Creamy Mayonnaise I

1. Place the rice milk, lemon juice, pepper, and xanthan gum in a blender. Blend on high speed about 1 minute or until foamy.

2. With the blender running on high speed, slowly add the oil one drop at a time through the opening in the lid. Continue for 5 minutes, or until about the half the oil has been added and the mixture begins to emulsify. At this point, you can begin to add the remaining oil in a very thin steady drip. Keep mixing until the mayonnaise is smooth and creamy. (It will be more liquidy than thick.) Add the salt and garlic (if using) and stir well.

3. Transfer the mayonnaise to an airtight container and refrigerate up to a week.

* Used as a thickening agent, xanthan gum is available in most natural foods stores.

Yield: About 1 cup

• • • • • • • •

$1/3$ cup cold rice milk

1 tablespoon lemon juice

$1/8$ teaspoon white pepper

$1/2$ teaspoon xanthan gum*

$1/4$ cup plus 2 tablespoons extra-virgin olive oil

$1/4$ cup plus 2 tablespoons safflower oil

1 small clove garlic, minced (optional)

$1/2$ teaspoon finely ground sea salt, or to taste

Dreamy Creamy Mayonnaise II

1. Place all the ingredients except the oil in a bowl and whisk until well blended. Transfer to a blender.

2. With the blender running on high speed, slowly add the oil one drop at a time through the opening in the lid. Continue for 5 minutes, or until about the half the oil has been added and the mixture begins to emulsify. At this point, you can begin to add the remaining oil in a very thin steady drip. Keep mixing until the mayonnaise is thick and creamy.

3. Transfer the mayonnaise to an airtight container and refrigerate up to a week.

Yield: About 1 cup

1 egg made with Ener-G-Egg-Replacer

1 tablespoon vinegar (rice, apple, and white wine are recommended)

1 teaspoon lemon juice

1 teaspoon agave nectar

1 small clove garlic, minced (optional)

$1/2$ teaspoon finely ground sea salt, or to taste

$1/4$ teaspoon dry mustard

1 cup safflower oil

Double-Delicious Bean Spread

Cannellini beans and chickpeas are blended together in this yummy spread.

1. Place all of the ingredients in a blender or food processor and blend until smooth.

2. Serve immediately or refrigerate and serve chilled. Store in the refrigerator up to five days.

Yield: About 2 cups

15-ounce can cannellini beans, rinsed and drained

15-ounce can chickpeas, rinsed and drained

1 small clove garlic, minced

$1/4$ cup lemon juice

3 tablespoons extra-virgin olive oil

$1/4$ teaspoon dried basil

Pinch black pepper

Crazy Mixed-Up Herb Pesto

*Traditional pesto is made with pine nuts and Parmesan cheese.
In this allergen-free version, dry roasted sunflower seeds
are used instead of pine nuts—
and it's so flavorful, the cheese will never be missed.*

Yield: About 1 ½ cups

• • • • • • • •

½ cup dry roasted
sunflower seeds

1 clove garlic, minced

1 ¼ cups loosely packed
fresh basil leaves

6 scallions, trimmed and
coarsely chopped

¼ cup fresh parsley leaves

2 tablespoons lemon juice

¼ teaspoon sea salt

3 tablespoons extra-virgin
olive oil

1. Place the sunflower seeds, garlic, basil, scallions, parsley, lemon juice, and sea salt in a food processor or blender. Process until the herbs are finely minced. With the motor running, add the olive oil slowly in a thin steady stream.

2. Transfer the mixture to a serving bowl.

3. Serve at room temperature with crackers and/or raw vegetables, or toss with rice pasta or other gluten-free variety. Store in the refrigerator up to five days.

CHANGE IT UP . . .

- Add 1 cup loosely packed fresh spinach leaves for increased nutritional value.

- For added flavor, blend a few pitted black olives with the other ingredients.

- If your child is not allergic to tree nuts, use dry-roasted pine nuts instead of sunflower seeds.

- If your child is able to eat dairy products, try stirring a tablespoon of grated Parmesan cheese into this pesto.

Velvety White Bean Dip

Fennel gives this creamy dip a mild licorice taste,
which appeals to many kids.
Perfect with raw veggies, crackers, or rice cakes.

Yield: About 3 cups
$1/4$ cup extra-virgin olive oil

1 clove garlic, minced

1 large fennel bulb, halved lengthwise, cored, and roughly chopped (reserve fronds for garnish)

$1/4$ cup water

15-ounce can white beans (Great Northern or cannellini), rinsed and drained

2 tablespoons lemon juice

1 teaspoon sea salt

$1/4$ teaspoon black pepper

1. Heat the oil in a medium frying pan over medium-low heat. Add the garlic and sauté 1 to 2 minutes, or until it becomes fragrant and turns golden brown around the edges.

2. Remove the garlic with a slotted spoon and place in a food processor or blender. Set aside.

3. Add the fennel to the frying pan and place over medium heat. Stirring occasionally, cook the fennel about 5 minutes or until it browns slightly around the edges and begins to smell sweet.

4. Add the water to the pan, bring to a simmer, and cook the fennel about 5 minutes, or until the water evaporates and the fennel is soft.

5. Transfer the fennel to the food processor along with the white beans, lemon juice, salt, and pepper. Purée until smooth and velvety.

6. Transfer the dip to a serving bowl and garnish with some of the feathery fennel fronds. Serve immediately or refrigerate and serve chilled. Store in the refrigerator up to five days.

CHANGE IT UP ...

- For a change, try making this dip with chickpeas instead of white beans.

Mummy's Yummy Hummus

*Packed with protein, fiber, vitamins, and minerals,
hummus is a versatile snack that kids can enjoy as a dip
with raw veggies, chips, and crackers,
as well as a delicious filling for pitas and tortillas.*

Yield: About 4 cups
• • • • • • •

$1/_2$ cup tahini
(sesame seed butter)

$1/_4$ cup extra-virgin
olive oil

$1/_4$ cup warm water

$1/_8$ cup lemon juice

2 cans (15 ounces each)
chickpeas, rinsed and
drained

2 small cloves garlic,
minced

$1/_2$ teaspoon ground cumin

$1/_2$ teaspoon sea salt

Pinch black pepper

1. Place the tahini, oil, water, and lemon juice in a blender or food processor and blend for 30 seconds.

2. Add half the chickpeas to the mixture and blend another 30 seconds. Add the remaining chickpeas and continue to blend until smooth.

3. Add the garlic, cumin, sea salt, and pepper, and blend an additional 10 seconds.

4. Transfer the mixture to a covered container and refrigerate at least 3 hours. Serve chilled. Store in the refrigerator up to five days.

CHANGE IT UP . . .

• For a nuttier flavored hummus, substitute sesame seed oil for the olive oil.

• Instead of raw garlic, use 3 roasted cloves for a milder flavored hummus.

• For a change, use white beans instead of chickpeas.

• For added texture and flavor, stir 2 tablespoons of finely chopped roasted red bell pepper or sun-dried tomatoes into the blended mixture.

Fun Freckled Sun Dip

Hey, this dip has freckles! Thanks to chopped black olives,
this sunflower based dip gets a fun freckled look
and a whole lot of flavor.

Yield: About 1 cup

• • • • • • •

1 cup sunflower seeds, soaked 8 hours or overnight

2 tablespoons lemon juice

1 tablespoon water

20 pitted black olives

1 scallion, finely chopped

1 small garlic clove, minced

2 teaspoons fresh thyme

$1/4$ teaspoon sea salt

1. Drain the soaked sunflower seeds, rinse under cold water, and drain again. Blot with paper towels to absorb excess water.

2. Transfer the seeds to a food processor along with the lemon juice and water. Process for 1 to 2 minutes, scraping down the sides of the processor frequently, until smooth.

3. Add 10 of the olives, the scallion, garlic, thyme, and salt, and continue to process another minute or until smooth and well blended. Transfer to a serving bowl.

4. Chop up the remaining olives and sprinkle over the dip.

5. Serve immediately or refrigerate and serve chilled. Store in the refrigerator up to five days.

JUST FOR FUN!

Get creative when adding sunflower butter, hummus, or thick bean spreads to rice cakes, crackers, or sliced fruit. Instead of spreading it on with a spoon or knife, try piping it on with a pastry bag. With just a few basic decorator tips, you can pipe the spreads into all sorts of fun shapes, scallops, and swirls. You can draw smiley faces, pipe your child's name, or write messages like "I ♥ You."

You can also use a pastry bag to fill snack cups like the Mini Crunch Cups on page 44, or to pipe filling into celery stalks or on top of halved cherry tomatoes.

Mini Crunch Cups

Noted vegan chef Vicki Chelf created the recipe for these tiny snack cups, which are prebaked and can be filled with all sorts of delicious snack foods—both sweet and savory.
Hummus and other thick spreads, creamy mashed avocado, and even applesauce or puréed fruit make great fillings!
Your kids can also use the cups as scoops to scoop up their favorite salsas or dips.
This recipe is also easily doubled.

Yield: 12 mini cups

- - - - - - -

$^3/_4$ cup rolled oats

$^1/_4$ cup flaxseed meal

$^1/_4$ teaspoon sea salt

1 tablespoon olive oil

3–4 tablespoons water

1. Preheat the oven to 350°F. Oil the 12 cups of a mini muffin tin and set aside.

2. Add the oats to a blender or food processor and grind for 25 to 30 seconds to form a coarse flour.

3. Add the flaxseed meal and sea salt to the blender and process with the oat flour about 15 to 20 seconds. Transfer to a medium mixing bowl.

4. Cut the olive oil into the flax-oat mixture with a fork until well distributed.

5. Stir the water into the mixture 1 tablespoon at a time until it becomes firm enough to hold a shape when pressed together with your hands. (Don't expect it to resemble a smooth kneadable dough. It will be somewhat coarse and crumbly.)

6. Press the mixture into a 12-inch long roll. Cut the roll into 12 pieces (1-inch long) and place one piece in each of the oiled muffin cups. Press the mixture on the bottom and sides of each cup in an even thickness (about $^1/_8$ inch).

7. Bake the cups for 18 to 20 minutes or until browned and crisp. Let cool about 5 minutes before removing from the tin. If necessary, run a knife around the edges to loosen.

8. Allow the cups to cool completely before filling. Store unfilled leftovers in an airtight container up to three days.

CHANGE IT UP . . .

- For a different flavor, add a tablespoon of sesame seeds, poppy seeds, or caraway seeds in Step 3.

- If using the cups for puréed fruit or other sweet filling, omit the salt and add $\frac{1}{2}$ teaspoon ground cinnamon in Step 3.

- For larger cups, double the recipe and bake in a standard muffin tin. This will yield 9 cups.

- When doubled, this recipe makes enough for a standard 9-inch pie crust, which you can either prebake or fill and bake like a conventional pie. Makes a great crust for quiche if your child is not allergic to eggs.

Chickpea Crunchies

A fantastic alternative to roasted nuts, this versatile snack is great to serve alone, tossed in a salad, or used as a garnish for soup.

1. Preheat the oven to 375°F.

2. Place the drained chickpeas on paper towels, pat them dry and place in a large bowl. Add the oil and salt, and toss the chickpeas until well coated.

3. Spread out the chickpeas on a baking sheet and bake for 15 to 20 minutes, or until browned and crunchy.

4. Serve warm or at room temperature.

Yield: About 1 $\frac{1}{2}$ cups

15-ounce can chickpeas, rinsed and drained

$\frac{1}{4}$ cup sunflower seed oil

1 teaspoon sea salt

CHANGE IT UP . . .

- For a spicy spark, add a few sprinkles of chili powder.

- Add $\frac{1}{2}$ teaspoon garlic powder for a garlicky version.

- For salty-sweet taste, blend 1 tablespoon of honey with the oil, and sprinkle the coated chickpeas with cinnamon.

Killer Kale Crisps

These mineral-rich chips are a crunchy alternative to potato chips.

Yield: 6 servings

• • • • • • •

12 ounces kale (1 large bunch), washed, stemmed, and chopped into 1-inch pieces

3 tablespoons extra-virgin olive oil

2 tablespoons apple cider vinegar

2 tablespoons honey

2 tablespoons garlic powder

1. Preheat the oven to 350°F.

2. Place the kale in a large bowl and set aside.

3. Whisk together the oil, cider, and honey, and pour over the kale. Toss well. Sprinkle with garlic powder and toss again.

4. Spread out the kale on a baking sheet in a single layer (you may have to do this in batches).

5. Place on a rack in the middle of the oven and bake 8 to 10 minutes. Toss the chips with a spatula and bake another 4 to 6 minutes or until crisp.

6. Serve warm or at room temperature.

EZ Potato Chips

There's no need to set up a deep fryer to make great potato chips. These oven-baked chips are crisp and delicious.

Yield: 6 to 8 servings

• • • • • • •

2 medium baking potatoes

3 tablespoons extra-virgin olive oil

1 teaspoon sea salt

1. Preheat oven to 400°F. Lightly oil a baking sheet and set aside.

2. Peel the potatoes and cut them into thin $1/8$-inch slices. You can do this with a sharp knife, a mandolin, or a hand grater with a wide cutting edge. Pat the slices with paper towels to remove excess moisture, then transfer to a large mixing bowl.

3. Drizzle the oil over the potatoes, then toss to coat. While tossing, sprinkle with salt.

4. Arrange the slices in a single layer on the prepared baking sheet. Bake for 15 minutes or until crisp and golden brown.

5. Serve hot from the oven, warm, or at room temperature. Store in an airtight container up to five days.

CHANGE IT UP . . .

- While tossing the potato slices, add 1 or 2 minced garlic cloves or $\frac{1}{2}$ teaspoon garlic powder.

Baked Tortilla Chips

Great to snack on all by themselves, these chips also go with just about any dip, spread, or salsa. And you can flavor them in lots of different kid-friendly ways (check out the Change It Up variations).

1. Preheat the oven to 375°F.

2. Coat both sides of the tortillas with oil, then cut each into 8 triangles. Place on a baking sheet and sprinkle with salt.

3. Bake for 10 to 12 minutes or until crisp.

4. Serve warm or at room temperature.

Yield: 80 crisps

· · · · · · ·

10 corn tortillas
(6-inch rounds)

2 tablespoons
extra-virgin olive oil

1 teaspoon sea salt

CHANGE IT UP . . .

- For a spicy spark, add a light sprinkling of chili powder before baking.

- Add $\frac{1}{2}$ teaspoon garlic powder before baking for a flavorful garlicky version.

- For lime-flavored chips, mix 2 tablespoons lime juice with the oil.

- For sweeter chips, mix 1 tablespoon pure maple syrup, agave nectar, or honey with the oil and sprinkle the chips with cinnamon instead of salt.

- Add 1 tablespoon balsamic vinegar to the oil for a tangy spark of flavor.

Chickpea Crackers

Although this recipe gives instructions for cutting these crackers into 1-inch squares, you can cut them into triangles, diamonds, or any shape you want. You can also use a cookie cutter to create other fun shapes like hearts or flowers. Kids love 'em!

Yield: About 20 crackers
• • • • • •

$^1/_2$ cup sifted
chickpea flour

2 tablespoons
nutritional yeast

$^1/_4$ teaspoon
baking powder

$^1/_4$ teaspoon sea salt

$^1/_8$ teaspoon turmeric

1 teaspoon extra-virgin
olive oil

2–4 tablespoons water

1. Combine the flour, nutritional yeast, baking powder, sea salt, and turmeric in a medium bowl.

2. While stirring, add the oil to the flour mixture, then begin adding the water 1 tablespoon at a time until a dough forms that can hold together.

3. Knead the dough several times until smooth and firm. Shape into a ball, cover with plastic wrap, and let rest for 10 minutes.

4. Preheat the oven to 350°F. Lightly oil a baking sheet and set aside.

5. Divide the rested dough in half. Place one of the halves on a clean work surface that is dusted with chickpea flour. Flatten the dough a bit with the palm of your hand and sprinkle the top with flour.

6. Using a rolling pin that has been dusted with flour, roll out the dough to about $^1/_4$-inch thickness. With a sharp knife, cut the dough into 1-inch squares and arrange on the prepared baking sheet.

7. Repeat with the remaining dough.

8. Before baking, prick the tops of the squares with the tines of a fork to prevent them from blistering and bubbling up as they bake.

9. Bake for 15 to 20 minutes, or until the tops are golden brown. Remove from the oven and let the crackers cool on the sheet. As they cool, they will become crisp. (Test one after it cools. If it isn't crisp, return the pan to the oven for a few more minutes.) Store in an airtight container up to a week.

CHANGE IT UP . . .

- Before baking the crackers, sprinkle them with flavorful herbs, spices, or seeds. Paprika, sesame seeds, poppy seeds, garlic powder, and even shredded coconut are just a few of the many options.

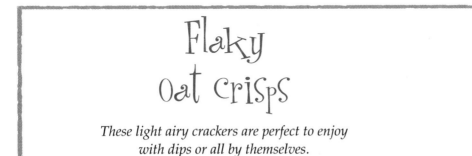

Flaky Oat Crisps

*These light airy crackers are perfect to enjoy
with dips or all by themselves.*

1. Preheat the oven to 350°F. Lightly oil a baking sheet and set aside.

2. Place the oats in a blender or food processor and grind to a coarse powder.

3. Transfer the oats to a large bowl, add the brown rice flour and sea salt, and stir until well combined.

4. While continuing to stir the flour, slowly add the olive oil until the mixture resembles coarse crumbs. Add the water and stir to form a ball of dough.

5. Knead the dough lightly, then roll or press it into a square or rectangle about $\frac{1}{8}$ inch thick. With a sharp knife or pizza cutter, cut the flattened dough into 2-inch squares.

6. Place the squares on the prepared baking sheet, and prick the tops with a fork to prevent them from blistering and bubbling up as they bake.

7. Bake the crackers for 12 to 15 minutes, or until the edges are slightly brown. Cool before serving.

Yield: 32 crackers

• • • • • • •

$1\frac{1}{2}$ cups rolled oats

1 cup brown rice flour

$\frac{1}{4}$ teaspoon sea salt

$\frac{1}{4}$ cup extra-virgin olive oil

$\frac{1}{2}$ cup water

Perfect Party Pita chips

These chips are perfect for dipping.
Serve them to your kids with Mummy's Yummy
Hummus (page 42) or any of the dips
and spreads in this chapter.

Yield: 48 chips

• • • • • • •

3 gluten-free/allergen-free
pita rounds (8-inches)

$^1/_2$ cup extra-virgin
olive oil

$^1/_2$ teaspoon sea salt

1. Preheat the oven to 400°F.

2. Brush both sides of the pita rounds with olive oil. Cut each round into eighths, then separate the tops and bottoms to form 16 triangles.

3. Sprinkle the triangles with salt and arrange on an unoiled baking sheet. Bake for 5 to 7 minutes or until lightly browned.

4. Serve hot from the oven, warm, or at room temperature. Store in an airtight container up to a week.

CHANGE IT UP . . .

- For savory flavored chips, sprinkle with herbs or spices before baking. Garlic powder, paprika, oregano, and turmeric are popular choices.

- For a sweeter pita chip, brush the rounds with grapeseed or sunflower oil instead of olive oil. Before baking, brush the triangles with a mixture of 2 tablespoons maple syrup, $^1/_2$ teaspoon cinnamon, and $^1/_4$ teaspoon nutmeg.

4

Cookies and Dessert Bars

What kid doesn't like coming home from school to find a plate of delicious cookies as an enjoyable mid-afternoon snack? Whether served during play dates, eaten as lunchbox treats, or enjoyed as after-dinner delights, cookies are always a welcomed choice.

In this chapter, we've shared an outstanding variety of cookies that are flavorful, delicious, and allergen-free. You will find classic choices, including two versions of oatmeal raisin cookies, as well as a few new innovations like Banana-Cranberry Oaties and our original Lemony Raspberry Muffies—a delicious cross between a cookie and a muffin. The light and chewy Lemon Drops are bursting with flavor, while the ever-popular Mrs. Marple's Maple Meltaways have a rich "peanut-buttery" taste—only without the peanuts. And if your kids like cinnamon, they are really going to enjoy the Pumpkin 'n Spice 'n Everything Nice Cookies, which are staples in our homes during the fall.

When it comes to no-bake varieties, we have included some that are sure to please, like the chewy Coco-Nutty Date Balls, the cool carob-flavored Thriller Chillers, and the super-crunchy Sunflower Butter Balls. Not only do kids enjoy eating these no-bake treats, they also love making them.

When it comes to snack appeal, brownies and other dessert-type bars can be as high on the list as cookies. And in this chapter you'll find our no-fail recipe for Carob Fudge Brownies, along with some favorite fruit-flavored bar treats.

Your kids are going to enjoy trying all the different snack choices in this chapter. We're hoping that some will become their favorites.

Pumpkin Eaters' Oatmeal Chewies

Pumpkin purée adds delicious flavor and moistness to these chewy cookies.

Yield: About 25 cookies

2 1/2 cups oat flour

1 tablespoon baking powder

1 tablespoon ground cinnamon

1 teaspoon ground nutmeg

2/3 cup rolled oats

1 cup raisins

1 cup pumpkin purée

1 cup pure maple syrup

1/2 cup grapeseed, safflower, or sunflower oil

1 teaspoon vanilla

1. Preheat the oven to 350°F. Lightly oil a cookie sheet and set aside.

2. Combine the flour, baking powder, cinnamon, and nutmeg in a medium bowl. Add the oats and raisins, and stir until well distributed. Set aside.

3. Place the pumpkin purée, oil, maple syrup, and vanilla in a large mixing bowl and stir until well blended.

4. Add the flour mixture to the pumpkin mixture and stir to form a firm rollable dough.

5. Roll the dough into 1-inch balls and place about 2 inches apart on the prepared cookie sheet. With your fingers or the bottom of a glass, flatten the balls to 1/2-inch thickness.

6. Bake for 10 to 12 minutes or until lightly browned.

7. Cool the cookies a few minutes before removing from the cookie sheet. Transfer to a wire rack to finish cooling. Serve warm or at room temperature.

CHANGE IT UP . . .

- Instead of raisins, use dried cranberries, currants, or diced dried apricots.

- For added crunch, add 1/2 cup raw pumpkin seeds.

- Using rice flour instead of oat flour will result in cookies that are a bit grainier but just as delicious.

Grand Ginger Cookies

*Aromatic ginger gives these cookies
just the right spark of flavor.*

1. Combine the flour, baking powder, and ground ginger in a medium bowl. Add the crystallized ginger and stir until well distributed. Set aside.

2. Place the date sugar, applesauce, oil, lemon juice, and vanilla in a large mixing bowl and stir until well blended.

3. Add the flour mixture to the applesauce mixture and stir to form a somewhat firm dough. Cover the bowl with plastic wrap and refrigerate at least 1 hour.

4. Preheat the oven to 350°F. Lightly oil a cookie sheet.

5. Roll the chilled dough into 1-inch balls and arrange about 2 inches apart on the prepared cookie sheet.

6. Bake for 10 to 12 minutes or until lightly browned.

7. Cool the cookies a few minutes before removing from the cookie sheet. Transfer to a wire rack to finish cooling. Serve warm or at room temperature.

Yield: About 20 cookies

• • • • • • •

3 cups brown rice flour

1 teaspoon baking powder

1 teaspoon ground ginger

$^3/_4$ cup minced crystallized ginger

1$^1/_4$ cups date sugar

$^1/_2$ cup applesauce

$^1/_4$ cup grapeseed, safflower, or sunflower oil

2 tablespoons lemon juice

1 teaspoon vanilla

CHANGE IT UP . . .

• For chocolate-flavored cookies, add $^1/_2$ cup carob powder.

• Add $^1/_2$ cup dried cranberries for added flavor, texture, and burst of color.

Pumpkin 'n Spice 'n Everything Nice Cookies

Light, flavorful, and a favorite among kids.

Yield: About 20 cookies

• • • • • • •

2 ½ cups brown rice flour

2 teaspoons baking powder

1 teaspoon ground cinnamon

½ teaspoon ground nutmeg

1 cup raisins

1 cup pumpkin purée

½ cup grapeseed, safflower, or sunflower oil

½ cup honey

1 teaspoon vanilla

1. Preheat the oven to 350°F. Lightly oil a cookie sheet and set aside.

2. Combine the flour, baking powder, cinnamon, and nutmeg in a medium bowl. Add the raisins and stir until well distributed. Set aside.

3. Place the pumpkin purée, oil, honey, and vanilla in a large mixing bowl and stir until well blended.

4. Add the flour mixture to the pumpkin mixture and stir to form a thick batter-like dough.

5. Drop rounded teaspoons of dough about 2 inches apart on the prepared cookie sheet.

6. Bake for 10 to 12 minutes or until lightly browned.

7. Cool the cookies a few minutes before removing from the cookie sheet. Transfer to a wire rack to finish cooling. Serve warm or at room temperature.

CHANGE IT UP . . .

• For smoother-textured cookies, use oat flour instead of rice flour.

Sesame Crunch Cookies

*A blend of crunchy sesame seeds and chewy dried fruit makes
this naturally sweet cookie a big hit with kids.*

1. Preheat the oven to 350°F. Lightly oil a cookie sheet and set aside.

2. Combine the flour, cinnamon, baking soda, nutmeg, cloves, and ginger in a medium bowl. Add the oats, sesame seeds, and raisins, and stir until well distributed. Set aside.

3. Place the orange juice, dates, and oil in a blender or food processor, and blend about 15 seconds or until smooth. Transfer to a large mixing bowl.

4. Add the flour mixture to the orange juice mixture and stir to form a thick batter-like dough.

5. Drop rounded tablespoons of dough about 2 inches apart on the prepared cookie sheet.

6. Bake for 10 to 12 minutes or until lightly browned.

7. Cool the cookies a few minutes before removing from the cookie sheet. Transfer to a wire rack to finish cooling. Serve warm or at room temperature.

Yield: About 24 cookies

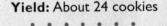

1 cup brown rice flour

1 tablespoon ground cinnamon

1 teaspoon baking soda

1/2 teaspoon ground nutmeg

1/4 teaspoon ground cloves

1/4 teaspoon ground ginger

3 cups rolled oats

1 cup sesame seeds

1 cup raisins

1 cup orange juice

1 cup chopped dates

3/4 cup grapeseed, safflower, or sunflower oil

Applesauce-Raisin Oatmeal Cookies

These great-tasting cookies are practically fat free!
They're also easy to make and bake up beautifully.

Yield: About 24 cookies

I cup brown rice flour

I teaspoon baking soda

I teaspoon ground cinnamon

$^1/_2$ teaspoon ground nutmeg

3 cups rolled oats

$^2/_3$ cup raisins

I cup applesauce

$^1/_2$ cup date sugar

I teaspoon vanilla

1. Preheat the oven to 350°F. Lightly oil a cookie sheet and set aside.

2. Combine the flour, baking soda, cinnamon, and nutmeg in a medium bowl. Add the oats and raisins and stir until well distributed. Set aside.

3. Place the applesauce, date sugar, and vanilla in a large mixing bowl and stir until well blended.

4. Add the flour mixture to the applesauce mixture and stir to form a firm rollable dough.

5. Roll the dough into 1-inch balls and place about 2 inches apart on the prepared cookie sheet. With your fingers or the bottom of a glass, flatten the balls to $^1/_4$-inch thickness.

6. Bake for 12 to 15 minutes or until lightly browned.

7. Cool the cookies a few minutes before removing from the cookie sheet. Transfer to a wire rack to finish cooling. Serve warm or at room temperature.

CHANGE IT UP . . .

- For maple-flavored cookies, use $^1/_4$ cup pure maple syrup instead of date sugar.

Banana-Cranberry Oaties

*This delicious cookie is one of our kids' favorite
after-school snacks.*

1. Preheat the oven to 350°F. Lightly oil a cookie sheet and set aside.

2. Combine the flour, baking powder, and cinnamon in a medium bowl. Add the oats and cranberries and stir until well distributed. Set aside.

3. Place the rice milk, oil, date sugar, and vanilla in a large mixing bowl and stir well. Add the bananas and continue to stir until well blended.

4. Add the flour mixture to the banana mixture and stir to form a thick batter-like dough.

5. Drop rounded tablespoons of dough about 2 inches apart on the prepared cookie sheet.

6. Bake for 12 to 15 minutes or until lightly browned.

7. Cool the cookies a few minutes before removing from the cookie sheet. Transfer to a wire rack to finish cooling. Serve warm or at room temperature.

Yield: About 12 cookies

1 cup oat flour

1 teaspoon baking powder

1 teaspoon ground cinnamon

$^3/_4$ cup rolled oats

$^1/_2$ cup dried cranberries

$^1/_3$ cup rice milk

$^1/_3$ cup safflower, sunflower, or grapeseed oil

$^1/_2$ cup date sugar

1 teaspoon vanilla

2 ripe bananas, mashed

Lemony Raspberry Muffies

*Years ago, we came across a recipe for lemon-raspberry muffins
that called for granulated sugar, buttermilk, and eggs.
We decided to experiment and make the recipe using date sugar
and rice milk, and skip the eggs altogether.
The fortunate result is what our families call "muffies"—
delicious sweet treats that are shaped like cookies
but have the texture of muffins.*

Yield: About 35 muffies
• • • • • • •

2 cups oat flour

1 cup date sugar

1 tablespoon baking powder

$1/2$ teaspoon sea salt (optional)

1 cup rice milk

$1/2$ cup grapeseed, safflower, or sunflower oil

$1/4$ cup lemon juice

$3/4$ cup fresh or frozen raspberries

1. Preheat the oven to 350°F. Lightly oil a cookie sheet and set aside.

2. Combine the flour, date sugar, baking powder, and salt (if using) in a large mixing bowl. Set aside.

3. Place the rice milk, oil, and lemon juice in a medium bowl and stir until well blended.

4. Add the rice milk mixture to the flour mixture and stir to form a thick batter.

5. Cut the raspberries in half (if using fresh), and carefully fold them into the batter.

6. Drop heaping tablespoons of batter about 2 inches apart on the prepared cookie sheet.

7. Bake for 10 to 12 minutes or until lightly browned.

8. Cool the muffies a few minutes before removing from the cookie sheet. Transfer to a wire rack to finish cooling. Serve warm or at room temperature.

Mrs. Marple's Maple Meltaways

These delicate melt-in-your-mouth cookies have a luscious "peanut buttery" taste without the peanuts.

1. Preheat the oven to 350°F. Lightly oil a cookie sheet and set aside.

2. Combine the flour and baking powder in a medium bowl and set aside.

3. Place the maple syrup, butter, oil, and vanilla in a large mixing bowl and stir until well blended.

4. Add the flour mixture to the maple mixture and stir to form a thick, sticky, batter-like dough.

5. Drop rounded tablespoons of dough about 2 inches apart on the prepared cookie sheet.

6. Bake for 10 to 12 minutes or until lightly browned.

7. Cool the cookies a few minutes before removing from the cookie sheet. Transfer to a wire rack to finish cooling. Serve warm or at room temperature.

Yield: About 30 cookies

2 cups oat flour

1 teaspoon baking powder

1 cup pure maple syrup

1 cup toasted sunflower seed butter

$1/3$ cup sunflower oil

1 tablespoon vanilla

CHANGE IT UP . . .

- For added crunch, sprinkle the cookies with raw sunflower seeds before baking.

- Use sesame seed butter instead of sunflower.

- For a spark of citrus flavor, add $1/4$ cup fresh lemon juice and some grated zest.

Outrageous Orange-Date Cookies

*Light and crisp, these orange-flavored cookies
get their delicate sweetness from dates.
Dates are also nutrient-rich and very satisfying—
their high-fiber content helps curb hunger pangs.*

Yield: About 20 cookies

I tablespoon flaxseed meal

2 tablespoons warm water

I cup brown rice flour

I teaspoon baking powder

I teaspoon ground
cinnamon

$^1/_2$ cup chopped dates

$^1/_2$ cup fresh orange juice

3 tablespoons grapeseed,
safflower, or sunflower oil

I teaspoon vanilla

1. Preheat the oven to 350°F. Lightly oil a cookie sheet and set aside.

2. In a cup or small bowl, mix together the flaxseed meal and water, and let sit for a minute.

3. Combine the flour, baking powder, and cinnamon in a medium mixing bowl. Add the dates and stir until well distributed. Set aside.

4. Place the orange juice, oil, vanilla, and flaxseed mixture in a large mixing bowl and stir until well blended.

5. Add the flour mixture to the juice mixture and stir to form a thick batter-like dough.

6. Drop rounded tablespoons of dough about 2 inches apart on the prepared cookie sheet.

7. Bake for 10 to 12 minutes or until lightly browned.

8. Cool the cookies a few minutes before removing from the cookie sheet. Transfer to a wire rack to finish cooling. Serve warm or at room temperature.

Ginger Maple Cookies

Fresh ginger is just one of the spotlighted flavors in these delicious spice cookies!

1. Preheat the oven to 350°F. Lightly oil a cookie sheet and set aside.

2. Combine the flour, baking powder, ground ginger, fresh ginger, cinnamon, nutmeg, cloves, and carob powder in a medium bowl. Set aside.

3. Place the maple syrup and oil in a large mixing bowl and stir until well blended.

4. Add the flour mixture to the maple mixture and stir to form a firm rollable dough.

5. Roll the dough into 1-inch balls and place about 2 inches apart on the prepared cookie sheet. With your fingers or the bottom of a glass, flatten the balls to $1/2$-inch thickness.

6. Bake for 10 to 12 minutes or until lightly browned.

7. Cool the cookies a few minutes before removing from the cookie sheet. Transfer to a wire rack to finish cooling. Serve warm or at room temperature.

Yield: About 30 cookies

• • • • • • •

3 cups brown rice flour

1 tablespoon baking powder

2 teaspoons ground ginger

2 tablespoons minced fresh ginger

1 tablespoon ground cinnamon

1 teaspoon ground nutmeg

$1/2$ teaspoon ground cloves

$1/3$ cup carob powder

1 cup pure maple syrup

$1/2$ cup grapeseed, safflower, or sunflower oil

Lemon Drops

These light chewy cookies are bursting with lemon flavor.

Yield: About 16 cookies

• • • • • • •

1 tablespoon flaxseed meal

2 tablespoons warm water

1 cup brown rice flour

1 teaspoon baking powder

$\frac{1}{2}$ cup unsweetened flaked coconut (optional)

$\frac{1}{2}$ cup lemon juice

3 tablespoons grapeseed, safflower, or sunflower oil

1 teaspoon vanilla

1. Preheat oven to 350°F. Lightly oil a cookie sheet and set aside.

2. In a cup or small bowl, mix together the flaxseed meal and water, and let sit for a minute.

3. Combine the flour, baking powder, and coconut (if using) in a medium bowl. Set aside.

4. Place the lemon juice, oil, vanilla, and flaxseed mixture in a large mixing bowl and stir until well blended.

5. Add the flour mixture to the lemon mixture and stir to form a thick batter-like dough.

6. Drop rounded tablespoons of dough about 2 inches apart on the prepared cookie sheet.

7. Bake for 10 to 12 minutes or until lightly browned.

8. Cool the cookies a few minutes before removing from the cookie sheet. Transfer to a wire rack to finish cooling.

JUST FOR FUN!

It's no secret that kids love fruit, and the fruit kabob is a great way for them to enjoy it. Threading a variety of different bite-sized fruits on a skewer (we use bamboo sticks or chopsticks) makes for a great kid-involved snacktivity—one that is perfect for parties and play dates. And nothing can be easier or more fun for kids. Just fill bowls with different fruits (our list of favorites is below), hand them a skewer, and let them create their fruity masterpieces. Fruit kabobs also freeze well (which is a real bonus since most kids tend to skewer more fruit than they can eat).

- Apple wedges
- Banana chunks
- Cantaloupe chunks
- Grapes
- Honeydew chunks
- Kiwi slices
- Mango chunks
- Orange sections
- Pear wedges
- Pineapple chunks
- Strawberries
- Watermelon chunks

Everyone's Favorite Oatmeal Raisin Cookies

Kids of all ages love this classic cookie.

1. Preheat the oven to 350°F. Lightly oil a cookie sheet and set aside.

2. Combine the flour, baking powder, and cinnamon in a medium bowl. Add the oats and raisins and stir until well distributed. Set aside.

3. Place the honey, oil, and vanilla in a large mixing bowl and stir until well blended.

4. Add the flour mixture to the honey mixture and stir to form a sticky batter-like dough.

5. Drop rounded tablespoons of dough about 2 inches apart on the prepared cookie sheet.

6. Bake for 10 to 12 minutes or until lightly browned.

7. Cool the cookies a few minutes before removing from the cookie sheet. Transfer to a wire rack to finish cooling. Serve warm or at room temperature.

Yield: About 30 cookies

• • • • • • •

$1\frac{1}{2}$ cups oat flour

1 teaspoon baking powder

1 tablespoon ground cinnamon

3 cups rolled oats

1 cup raisins

1 cup honey

$\frac{2}{3}$ cup grapeseed, safflower, or sunflower oil

1 tablespoon vanilla

CHANGE IT UP . . .

• For added flavor and texture, add 1 cup of sunflower seeds or unsweetened shredded coconut.

• For a chewy, moister cookie, substitute the oil with an equal amount of applesauce.

• Olive oil's distinctive taste is generally not suitable for baked goods, but it works in this recipe. When using olive oil, reduce the honey to $\frac{3}{4}$ cup and add $\frac{1}{3}$ cup pure maple syrup for a sweeter taste.

Sunflower Butter Balls

Yield: About 20 balls

2 cups dry roasted
sunflower seeds

I cup oat flour

$1/4$ cup flaxseed meal

I teaspoon ground
cinnamon

$1/2$ teaspoon ground
nutmeg

2 tablespoons honey

$2/3$ cup applesauce

*Not only do kids find these crunchy no-bake snacks delicious,
they love making them!*

1. Place the sunflower seeds in a food processor and process to a smooth butter.

2. Add the flour, flaxseed meal, cinnamon, nutmeg, and honey, and blend until the mixture holds together.

3. Transfer the mixture to a large bowl, add the applesauce, and stir to form a firm sticky dough.

4. Roll the mixture into 1-inch balls and place on a cookie sheet. Cover and refrigerate at least 2 hours. Serve chilled.

Puffed Rice and Raisin Treats

Yield: About 12 treats

I cup sunflower seed
butter

3 tablespoons honey

$1/4$ cup raisins

I teaspoon ground
cinnamon

$3/4$ cup puffed rice cereal

*This no-bake honey-sweetened snack is a little sticky,
but fun to make and eat.*

1. Place the sunflower butter, honey, raisins, and cinnamon in a large mixing bowl and stir until well blended. Add the puffed rice and mix until well coated.

2. Form the mixture into 1-inch balls and arrange on a plate or serving platter.

3. Serve immediately or refrigerate and serve chilled.

CHANGE IT UP . . .

- Add 1 tablespoon roasted carob powder for a chocolatey flavor.

Carob Sunflower Balls

*Offer kids these crunchy bite-sized treats
for a quick burst of energy.*

Yield: About 24 balls

1. Preheat the oven to 350°F. Lightly oil a cookie sheet and set aside.

2. Combine the flour, sunflower seeds, puffed rice, and cinnamon in a medium bowl. Set aside.

3. Place the carob powder, oil, and sunflower butter in a small bowl and stir until smooth. Add the water and honey, and continue to stir until well blended. Pour over the flour mixture and stir until well combined.

4. Roll the mixture into 1-inch balls and place about an inch or so apart on the prepared cookie sheet.

5. Bake for 8 to 10 minutes or until lightly browned.

6. Serve warm or at room temperature.

I cup brown rice flour

$3/4$ cup toasted sunflower seeds

I cup puffed rice cereal

I teaspoon ground cinnamon

$3/4$ cup roasted carob powder

$1/4$ cup sunflower or sesame oil

$1/4$ cup toasted sunflower seed butter

$1/2$ cup water

$1/4$ cup honey

Coco-nutty Date Balls

*Vitamin- and mineral-rich dates provide the sweetness
for these delicious no-bake treats.*

Yield: About 12 balls

1. Place all of the ingredients in a food processor and grind until the mixture is slightly grainy in texture. Transfer to a mixing bowl.

2. Roll the mixture into 1-inch balls and arrange on a plate or serving platter.

3. Serve immediately or refrigerate and serve chilled.

3 cups pitted dates

$1/2$ cup roasted carob powder

$1/2$ cup unsweetened shredded coconut

I teaspoon ground cinnamon

I teaspoon vanilla

Thriller Chillers

These chilled, slightly chewy sweet treats are a snap to make.

Yield: About 25 balls

• • • • • • •

$^1/_4$ cup agave nectar

$^3/_4$ cup warm water

2 cups dry roasted
sunflower seeds

I tablespoons
flaxseed meal

I tablespoon vanilla

$^3/_4$ cup carob powder

$^1/_2$ cup finely chopped
dates

I teaspoon ground
cinnamon

1. In a small bowl, mix together the agave and water, and set aside.

2. Place the sunflower seeds in a blender and grind to a powdery meal. Transfer to a medium mixing bowl.

3. Add the flaxseed meal and vanilla to the agave-water mixture and stir well. Add to the ground sunflower seeds along with the remaining ingredients. Mix until well combined.

4. Roll the mixture into 1-inch balls and place on a cookie sheet or platter. Cover and refrigerate at least 3 hours. Serve chilled.

CHANGE IT UP . . .

• After forming the balls, roll them in unsweetened shredded coconut.

JUST FOR FUN!

How about offering your kids an apple "bagel" for a quick and easy anytime snack?

After coring a large apple (we like Granny Smith) cut away about $^1/_2$-inch from the top and bottom. Cut the remaining apple into 4 equally thick rounds. Top 2 rounds with a layer of sunflower seed butter, then sprinkle with one or more of the following goodies:

dried cranberries	raisins
shredded coconut	grated carrots
sliced strawberries	sunflower seeds

Cover with the remaining apple slices and voila . . . delicious (and nutritious) apple bagels! As a variation, you can make pineapple bagels using pineapple rings.

Jammin' Blueberry Bliss Bars

Fruit-sweetened jam gives these delicious snack bars just the right touch of sweetness.

Yield: 12 bars

• • • • • • •

1³/₄ cups quinoa flour

1 teaspoon baking soda

1 teaspoon ground cinnamon

1¹/₂ cups rolled oats

¹/₂ cup grapeseed, safflower, or sunflower oil

¹/₂ cup honey

¹/₂ cup water

1 teaspoon vanilla

1 cup unsweetened blueberry jam

1. Preheat the oven to 350°F. Lightly oil an 11-x-7-inch baking pan and set aside.

2. Combine the flour, baking soda, and cinnamon in a medium bowl. Add the oats and stir until well distributed. Set aside.

3. Place the oil, honey, water, and vanilla in a large mixing bowl and stir until well-blended.

4. Add the flour mixture to the honey mixture and stir to form a thick batter.

5. Spoon half the batter in an even layer on the bottom of the prepared baking pan.

6. Spread the jam over the batter, then cover with the remaining batter.

7. Bake for 20 to 25 minutes or until the top is slightly browned. Remove the pan from the oven and place on a wire rack to cool.

8. Cool at least 10 minutes before cutting into bars and serving.

CHANGE IT UP . . .

• Instead of quinoa flour, try an equal amount of buckwheat, brown rice, or teff flour. ·

• Use any unsweetened berry jam.

Scrumptious Strawberry Bars

Strawberry preserves add delicious sweet flavor to these chewy cookie bars, but any preserves will work.

Yield: 20 bars

• • • • • • • •

1³/₄ cups brown rice flour

1 cup rolled oats

³/₄ cup date sugar

¹/₂ cup sunflower seeds

1 teaspoon baking powder

¹/₂ cup applesauce

¹/₃ cup grapeseed, safflower, or sunflower oil

1¹/₂ cups unsweetened strawberry preserves

1. Preheat the oven to 350°F. Lightly oil an 11-x-7-inch baking pan and set aside.

2. Combine the flour, oats, date sugar, sunflower seeds, and baking powder in a large mixing bowl. Add the applesauce and oil, and stir to form a thick batter.

3. Measure 1 cup of the batter and set aside.

4. Spoon the remaining batter on the bottom of the prepared pan. Bake for 15 to 20 minutes or until lightly browned. Remove from the oven.

5. Carefully spread the strawberry preserves in an even layer over the hot crust. Sprinkle the reserved batter over the preserves and bake another 15 to 20 minutes or until the crust is browned and the preserves are bubbling. Remove the pan from the oven and place on a wire rack to cool.

6. Cool at least 10 minutes before cutting into bars and serving.

Figgle-Giggle Squares

These high-fiber treats are sweet, chewy, and filling.

1. Preheat the oven to 350°F. Lightly oil an 8-inch square baking pan and set aside.

2. Place the figs in a small saucepan, cover with water, and bring to a boil. Turn off the heat and allow the figs to soak 7 to 10 minutes to soften.

3. While the figs are soaking, combine the flour, oats, and baking soda in a medium bowl. Set aside.

4. Place the honey, rice milk, and oil in a large mixing bowl and stir until well blended. Add the flour mixture and stir to form a thick batter.

5. Drain the softened figs and transfer to a blender or food processor. Add the lukewarm water and purée about 1 minute or until smooth.

6. Spoon slightly more than half the batter in the bottom of the prepared pan. Spread the puréed figs in an even layer on top, then cover with the remaining batter. Pat slightly to flatten.

7. Bake for 15 to 20 minutes or until top is lightly browned. Remove the pan from the oven and place on a wire rack to cool.

8. Cool for at least 10 minutes before cutting into squares and serving.

Yield: 12 squares
• • • • • • •
26 dried figs

2 cups brown rice flour

$^3/_4$ cup rolled oats

1 teaspoon baking soda

$^1/_2$ cup honey

$^1/_2$ cup rice milk

$^1/_4$ cup grapeseed, safflower, or sunflower oil

4 tablespoons lukewarm water

Carob Fudge Brownies

*We always make a double batch of these moist, delicious brownies—
one to enjoy right away, and another to freeze and snack on later.
Our kids even like them while they're still frozen!*

Yield: 12 brownies

• • • • • • •

2$^{1}/_{2}$ cups oat flour

$^{3}/_{4}$ cup carob powder

1 teaspoon baking powder

1$^{3}/_{4}$ cups honey

$^{3}/_{4}$ cup water

$^{3}/_{4}$ cup grapeseed,
safflower, or sunflower oil

1 teaspoon vanilla

1. Preheat the oven to 350°F. Lightly oil a 13-x-9-inch baking pan and set aside.

2. Combine the flour, carob powder, and baking powder in a medium bowl. Set aside.

3. Place the honey, water, oil, and vanilla in a large mixing bowl and stir until well blended.

4. Add the flour mixture to the honey mixture and stir to form a smooth batter. Spoon the batter into the prepared pan and spread in an even layer.

5. Bake for 20 to 25 minutes or until a toothpick inserted into the middle of the brownie comes out clean. Remove the pan from the oven and place on a wire rack to cool.

6. Cool at least 10 minutes before cutting the brownie into squares and serving.

CHANGE IT UP . . .

• Instead of oat flour, try an equal amount of quinoa, rice, or teff flour.

• For added flavor and texture, add $^{1}/_{3}$ cup raisins or $^{1}/_{2}$ cup sunflower seeds to the batter.

• Instead of oil, you can use $^{2}/_{3}$ cup applesauce.

• For a sweet maple flavor, substitute 1$^{1}/_{2}$ cups pure maple syrup for the honey.

5

Muffins and Other Sweet Treats

Mmmm . . . there's nothing like the heavenly aroma of muffins baking in the oven. It's practically irresistible. Muffins have long been considered favorite treats, and because they can be made with healthful ingredients, they are great snack choices for kids (with or without food allergies).

The muffins in this chapter—made with cornmeal, brown rice flour, oat flour, teff flour, and/or flaxseed meal—are gluten-free. They call for unsaturated oils like safflower, sunflower, and grapeseed; as well as nutritious whole fruits and other high-fiber ingredients. When it comes to sweeteners, natural unprocessed (or minimally processed) products like pure maple syrup, honey, and date sugar are used. And talk about fun and flavorful extras. Raisins, dried cranberries, currants, and chopped dates are just a few of the goodies that add to the "delcious-ness" of our muffins. As an added bonus, the recipes are easy and can be made in a snap—

from start to finish most can be prepared in under thirty minutes.

Although all of the recipes in this chapter give instructions for standard-size ($2\,^3/_4$ inch) muffins, you can also use the batter to make jumbo or mini varieties. A recipe that yields twelve standard muffins also makes six jumbo (3 inch) or thirty-two mini ($1\,^1/_2$ inch) muffins.

Along with muffins, this chapter also includes a number of other popular sweet treats that kids really love. You will find perfect take-along choices like the No-Fail Trail Mix and Sunny Granola Crunch, which also makes a terrific breakfast cereal. Colorful Confetti Popcorn Balls are fun to make and eat, while the easy-to-prepare Carob Fudge Squares can be frozen to enjoy later. There are also recipes for puddings, fruity tortilla roll-ups, luscious sorbet, and much more. We're betting that your kids will enjoy trying them all.

classic Blueberry Muffins

Rich in beneficial antioxidants, fresh blueberries take the spotlight in these classic muffins.

Yield: 10 muffins

● ● ● ● ● ● ● ●

2 cups brown rice flour

1 teaspoon baking powder

1 teaspoon ground cinnamon

2 cups fresh or frozen blueberries*

1 cup honey

1/2 cup rice milk

1/2 cup applesauce

1/4 cup grapeseed, safflower, or sunflower oil

1 teaspoon vanilla

* If using frozen, rinse, drain, and pat dry.

1. Preheat the oven to 350°F.

2. Combine the flour, baking powder, and cinnamon in a medium bowl. Add the blueberries and stir until well distributed.

3. Place the honey, rice milk, applesauce, oil, and vanilla in a large bowl and stir until well blended.

4. Add the flour mixture to the honey mixture and stir to form a thick batter.

5. Spoon about 2 heaping tablespoons of batter into the cups of a greased or paper-lined standard muffin tin.

6. Bake for 20 to 25 minutes or until a toothpick inserted into the center of a muffin comes out clean.

7. Cool the muffins at least 10 minutes before removing from the tin.

THE MIGHTY BLUEBERRY

They may be tiny, but blueberries sure pack a mighty punch when it comes to health benefits. Compared to other fruits, they are the richest source of cancer-fighting antioxidants. Low in calories and virtually fat-free, blueberries also contain a good amount of vitamin C and dietary fiber. Even when frozen, these mildly sweet superstars retain their beneficial nutrients. They rank second behind strawberries as the most commonly eaten berry in the United States, and are one of the few fruits that are native to North America.

When buying fresh blueberries, choose those that are plump and uniform in color, which can range from deep blue to dark purple. Avoid berries that are soft and mushy or dried and wrinkled. Also keep an eye out for damaged berries or the presence of mold. Like most berries, blueberries are highly perishable. Before buying frozen varieties, shake the bag gently to make sure the berries are loose. If they are clumped together in a frozen mass they may have been thawed and refrozen.

Pineapple Cornbread Muffins

Adding juicy pineapple to an already-delicious corn muffin makes it a doubly delightful treat.

1. Preheat the oven to 350°F.

2. Combine the cornmeal, flour, and baking powder in a medium bowl.

3. Place the honey, rice milk, oil, and vinegar in a large bowl and stir until well blended. Add the pineapple and stir well.

4. Add the flour mixture to the honey mixture and stir to form a thick batter.

5. Spoon about 2 heaping tablespoons of batter into the cups of a greased or paper-lined standard muffin tin.

6. Bake for 20 to 25 minutes or until a toothpick inserted into the center of a muffin comes out clean.

7. Cool the muffins at least 10 minutes before removing from the tin.

Yield: 10 muffins

• • • • • • •

1 1/2 cups cornmeal

2 cups brown rice flour

1 teaspoon baking powder

3/4 cup honey

3/4 cup rice milk

1/4 cup grapeseed, safflower, or sunflower oil

1 teaspoon apple cider vinegar

20-ounce can crushed pineapple, drained

Perfectly Perfect Pear Muffins

Made from world's tiniest grain, teff flour lends a sweet malty flavor to these delicious muffins.

Yield: 10 muffins

1 ¹/₂ cups teff flour

1 teaspoon baking powder

1 teaspoon ground cinnamon

2 bosc pears, peeled and cut into small pieces

1 cup chopped dates

1 cup applesauce

³/₄ cup sunflower seed butter

²/₃ cup honey

1 teaspoon vanilla

1. Preheat the oven to 350°F.

2. Combine the flour, baking powder, and cinnamon in a medium bowl. Add the pears and dates and stir until well distributed. Set aside.

3. Place the applesauce, sunflower butter, honey, and vanilla in a large bowl and stir until well blended.

4. Add the flour mixture to the applesauce mixture and stir to form a thick batter.

5. Spoon about 2 heaping tablespoons of batter into the cups of a greased or paper-lined standard muffin tin.

6. Bake for 20 to 25 minutes or until a toothpick inserted into the center of a muffin comes out clean.

7. Cool the muffins at least 10 minutes before removing from the tin.

CHANGE IT UP . . .

- Instead of teff flour, try this recipe with oat or quinoa flour.
- Substitute dried cranberries, currants, or chopped golden raisins for the dates.

Pumpkin Patch Muffins

*On Thanksgiving and Halloween, you can always find
these muffins in our homes.*

1. Preheat the oven to 350°F.

2. Combine the flour, baking powder, cinnamon, and nutmeg in
a medium bowl. Add the raisins and pumpkin seeds (if using)
and stir until well distributed. Set aside.

3. Place the purée, honey, rice milk, and oil in a large mixing bowl
and stir until well blended.

4. Add the flour mixture to the purée-honey mixture and stir to
form a thick batter.

5. Spoon about 2 heaping tablespoons of batter into the cups of
a greased or paper-lined standard muffin tin.

6. Bake for 20 to 25 minutes or until a toothpick inserted into the
center of a muffin comes out clean.

7. Cool the muffins at least 10 minutes before removing from
the tin.

Yield: 12 muffins
• • • • • • • •
2 cups brown rice flour

1 teaspoon baking powder

1 teaspoon ground
cinnamon

1 teaspoon ground nutmeg

$1/2$ cup raisins

$1/2$ cup pumpkin seeds
(optional)

$3/4$ cup pumpkin purée

$1/2$ cup honey

$1/2$ cup rice milk

$1/4$ cup grapeseed,
safflower, or sunflower oil

Annie's
Apple Oat Muffins

Moist and not too sweet, these fruit-filled muffins
are loaded with flavor.

Yield: 12 muffins

- - - - - - -

1 tablespoon flaxseed meal

2 tablespoons warm water

1 cup oat flour

¹/₂ cup oat bran

1 tablespoon
ground cinnamon

1 teaspoon baking powder

1 large Granny Smith or
other green apple, peeled
and shredded

¹/₂ cup raisins

¹/₃ cup applesauce

¹/₄ cup grapeseed,
safflower, or sunflower oil

¹/₄ cup honey

1. Preheat the oven to 350°F.

2. In a cup or small bowl, mix together the flaxseed meal and water, and let sit for a minute.

3. Combine the flour, bran, cinnamon, and baking powder in a medium bowl. Add the apple and raisins and stir until well distributed. Set aside.

4. Place the applesauce, oil, honey, and flaxseed mixture in a large bowl and stir until well blended.

5. Add the flour mixture to the applesauce mixture and stir to form a thick batter.

6. Spoon about 2 heaping tablespoons of batter into the cups of a greased or paper-lined standard muffin tin.

7. Bake for 20 to 25 minutes or until a toothpick inserted into the center of a muffin comes out clean.

8. Cool the muffins at least 10 minutes before removing from the tin.

CHANGE IT UP . . .

- For a nuttier flavor, substitute quinoa or teff flour for the oat flour.

Banana Currant Muffins

*Often dried and used like raisins in baking, tiny currants
are rich in calcium, iron, and vitamin C.
They add a delicate sweet, slightly tart flavor to these muffins.*

Yield: 10 muffins

2 cups oat flour

1 tablespoon baking powder

1 teaspoon ground cinnamon

$\frac{1}{2}$ cup dried currants

3 ripe bananas, mashed

$\frac{1}{2}$ cup honey

$\frac{1}{4}$ cup water

$\frac{1}{4}$ cup sunflower oil

1 teaspoon vanilla

1. Preheat the oven to 350°F.

2. Combine the flour, baking powder, and cinnamon in a medium bowl. Add the currants and stir until well distributed. Set aside.

3. Place the bananas, honey, water, oil, and vanilla in a large mixing bowl and stir until well blended.

4. Add the flour mixture to the banana mixture and stir to form a thick batter.

5. Spoon about 2 heaping tablespoons of batter into the cups of a greased or paper-lined standard muffin tin.

6. Bake for 20 to 25 minutes or until a toothpick inserted into the center of a muffin comes out clean.

7. Cool the muffins at least 10 minutes before removing from the tin.

CHANGE IT UP . . .

- For a nuttier flavor, substitute quinoa or teff flour for the oat flour.

- Instead of currants, use dried cranberries or chopped raisins.

Apple Blueberry Crisp

Blueberries are delicious raw or cooked, and they add sweet flavor to this delicious crisp.

Yield: 4 to 6 servings

5 cups peeled, thinly sliced Granny Smith or other green apple

1 cup fresh or frozen blueberries*

$^2/_3$ cup rolled oats

$^1/_4$ cup date sugar

2 tablespoons brown rice flour

1 teaspoon ground cinnamon

3 tablespoons grapeseed, safflower, or sunflower oil

* If using frozen, rinse, drain, and pat dry.

1. Preheat the oven to 375°F.

2. Place the apples and blueberries in an unoiled 2-quart baking dish and set aside.

3. Combine all of the remaining ingredients except the oil in a medium mixing bowl. Drizzle the oil over the mixture, then cut it in with a fork.

4. Sprinkle the oat mixture over the apples and blueberries.

5. Bake for 30 to 35 minutes or until the topping is browned and crisp.

6. Serve warm or at room temperature.

Franny's Frozen Banana Dessert

This frozen treat is perfect to enjoy on a hot summer afternoon.

Yield: 4 servings

6 ripe bananas

2 tablespoons pure maple syrup

2 tablespoons carob powder

1 tablespoon vanilla

1 teaspoon ground cinnamon

1. Place all of the ingredients in a blender or food processor and blend until smooth.

2. Spoon the mixture into freezer-safe cups or small bowls, cover, and place in the freezer until firm.

3. Before serving, let sit a few minutes to thaw a bit.

Granny's Apple Crisp

For this recipe, green apple varieties like Granny Smith or Pippin are the best (organic, of course).

1. Preheat the oven to 350°F. Lightly oil a 9-inch square baking dish and set aside.

2. Combine all of the ingredients except the apples in a large bowl. Set aside.

3. Place the apples in the bottom of the prepared baking pan and cover with the oat mixture.

4. Bake for 50 to 55 minutes or until the topping is browned and crisp.

5. Serve warm or at room temperature.

Yield: 4 servings

$^1/_2$ cup rolled oats

$^1/_2$ cup oat flour

$^1/_2$ cup pure maple syrup

$^1/_3$ cup grapeseed, safflower, or sunflower oil

1 teaspoon ground cinnamon

1 teaspoon vanilla

4 cups unpeeled, diced Granny Smith or other green apple

Maple Cinnamon Applesauce

The best time to make applesauce is in the fall, when apples are at their seasonal peak. Pure maple syrup complements the apples in this recipe.

1. Peel the apples and cut into 1-inch chunks.

2. Place the apples and water in a large pot and bring to a boil over medium-high heat. Reduce the heat to low, cover, and simmer the apples for 25 to 30 minutes or until soft. Transfer to a large mixing bowl.

3. Mash the apples to the desired consistency. Add the maple syrup and cinnamon, and stir until well blended.

4. Serve warm or refrigerate and serve chilled.

Yield: 4 servings

6 large McIntosh, Granny Smith, or other tart apples

2 large Golden Delicious or other sweet apples

$^1/_4$ cup water

2 tablespoons pure maple syrup

1 teaspoon ground cinnamon

Quinoa Raisin Pudding

Yield: 2 servings

. . . .

1 cup quinoa, rinsed
and drained

2 cups water

2 cups apple juice

1 cup raisins

2 tablespoons lemon juice

1 teaspoon ground
cinnamon

$\frac{1}{2}$ teaspoon ground
nutmeg

1 tablespoon vanilla

*Although nutty-flavored gluten-free quinoa (KEEN-wah) is referred to as
a grain—and cooked and eaten like one—it is actually a seed.
It's a great choice to use in this delicious pudding.*

1. Place the quinoa and water in a medium pot, stir once, and
bring to a boil over medium-high heat. Reduce heat to low,
cover, and simmer 10 minutes or until the water is absorbed.

2. Add all of the remaining ingredients except the vanilla to the
pot. Cover and simmer another 8 minutes or until the pudding
thickens and becomes slightly creamy. Add the vanilla and
stir well.

3. Serve warm or refrigerate and serve chilled.

Purple Pudding

Yield: 2 to 3 servings

. . . .

2 cups water

1 cup black rice

1 cup unsweetened
coconut milk

3 tablespoons
finely chopped
crystallized ginger

3 tablespoons date sugar

*The nutrient-rich black rice that is used in this pudding
actually turns purple when cooked. Flavored with
coconut milk and bits of crystallized ginger, this snack
is a fun and delicious alternative to yogurt or ice cream.*

1. Bring the water to boil in a heavy 2-quart pot over medium-
high heat. Add the rice and return to a boil. Stir once, cover the
pot, and simmer over low heat for 30 minutes or until the rice
is soft and almost cooked.

2. Add the remaining ingredients, increase the heat to medium-
high and bring to a boil. Reduce the heat to maintain a low
boil. Stirring occasionally, continue to cook for 12 to 15 minutes
or until the pudding thickens.

3. Serve warm or refrigerate and serve chilled.

CHANGE IT UP . . .

- For a "non-purple" version of this pudding, use brown or wild rice instead of black rice. If using brown rice, continue cooking for 8 to 10 minutes in Step 2. For wild rice, continue cooking for 10 to 20 minutes.

JUST FOR FUN!

Most kids find it irresistible to pass up any food or beverage that's served in an unconventional way. Whether it's strawberries in a martini glass, vegetable sticks in a Chinese food takeout box, or cereal in a giant coffee mug, presentation really is everything. Craft stores and dollar stores are filled with items that can be used for creative serving and decorating—colorful plates and bowls; jars, glasses, and cups of all shapes and sizes; small cardboard boxes and containers; and eye-catching paper gift bags are just a few standard items you'll find while browsing the shelves. You probably already own things that you can use as well. Here are a few fun, creative ways to serve snacks to your kids:

- Serve popcorn in a cone-shaped party hat or colorful gift bag.

- Fill two or three cups of a standard muffin tin with spreads or dips. Fill the remaining cups with a variety of raw vegetables like cherry tomatoes, pitted olives, broccoli florets, and rounds of cucumber, carrot, and zucchini. Fun for play dates.

- Hollow out bell peppers to serve as bowls. Fill them with colorful vegetable sticks for dipping or with the dips themselves.

- Fill a gluten-free ice cream cone with fresh berries or granola.

- Thread chunks of fruit or vegetables on toothpicks, then skewer them into a pineapple or grapefruit for a festive party centerpiece.

- Hollow out half of a small watermelon and fill it with fresh berries and bite-sized pieces of melon. Offer chopsticks and/or toothpicks to spear the fruit. Good for parties.

- Create a "carrot patch" by filling a clean plastic-lined clay flower pot with bean dip and "planting" baby carrots on top by sticking them partially into the dip.

- Serve smoothies and other beverages with colorful flex straws or crazy straws, and garnish with a fruit that is used in the drink.

Carob Fudge Squares

*This fudge is easy to make, requires no baking,
and is a great snack food.*

Yield: About 30 pieces
(1-inch squares)
• • • • • • •

1 cup apple juice

4 tablespoons agar flakes

$\frac{1}{2}$ cup maple syrup

$\frac{1}{2}$ cup carob powder

$\frac{1}{2}$ cup tahini

1 tablespoon vanilla

1. Lightly oil a 6-x-8-inch glass baking dish and set aside.

2. Place $\frac{1}{2}$ cup of the apple juice, the agar, and maple syrup in a medium pot and bring to a boil over medium-high heat. Reduce the heat to low and simmer 2 to 3 minutes or until the agar dissolves and the mixture is clear.

3. Add the carob powder, tahini, and remaining apple juice to the pot. Stirring gently, cook the mixture another minute or until it is thick and somewhat sticky. Add the vanilla and stir well.

4. Spoon the mixture into the prepared pan, and pat down into a smooth even layer with your hand. Cover with plastic wrap and refrigerate at least 30 minutes or until firm.

5. Cut into 1-inch squares and serve. Store in an airtight container and refrigerate for three to five days, or freeze up to three months.

Carob Halvah

Yield: 8 servings
• • • • • • •

$\frac{1}{2}$ cup unsweetened
flaked coconut

$\frac{1}{2}$ cup ground dry roasted
sunflower seeds

$\frac{1}{2}$ cup oat bran

$\frac{1}{4}$ cup carob powder

$\frac{2}{3}$ cup tahini

$\frac{1}{3}$ cup honey

*Although there are many variations of this Middle Eastern candy,
the classic recipe consists primarily of ground sesame seeds and
honey. Our version also contains sunflower seeds
and coconut, and is flavored with carob.*

1. Place all of the ingredients in a large bowl and stir until well combined.

2. Divide the mixture in half and place each half on a sheet of wax paper.

3. Roll each half into a 1-inch-thick roll and seal in the wax paper.

4. Refrigerate at least 2 hours or until firm.

5. When ready to serve, unwrap the roll and cut into slices as desired. Rewrap any leftover halvah and refrigerate up to a week.

CHANGE IT UP . . .

- Omit the carob powder.
- Instead of sunflower seeds, try dry roasted pumpkin seeds.

Super Strawberry Roll Ups

The sky is practically the limit when it comes to the number of different fillings you can use in this easy-to-assemble snack.

1. On each tortilla, spread 3 tablespoons of sunflower butter.

2. Spread 2 tablespoons of jam in an even layer over the butter.

3. Top each tortilla with chopped strawberries.

4. Roll up the tortillas and serve.

CHANGE IT UP . . .

- For sesame flavored roll ups, use tahini instead of sunflower seed butter.
- Instead of strawberries, use blueberries or raspberries.

Yield: 4 roll ups

4 corn or brown rice tortillas (6-inch rounds)

$3/4$ cup dry roasted sunflower seed butter

$1/2$ cup unsweetened fruit-only strawberry jam

I cup finely chopped strawberries

FROZEN QUICK BITES

When it comes to the kind of snacks that most parents give their kids, fruit tops the list. Kids love all types of fruit, which is why it's a good idea always to have some on hand.

Freezing fresh berries or chunks of whole fruit is one way to turn an already delicious snack into frosty bite-sized treats. With very little effort—as shown in the tips below—you can freeze any of the following fruits to satisfy an unexpected snack attack at a moment's notice.

- Apple slices
- Apricot slices
- Banana slices
- Blackberries
- Blueberries
- Cantaloupe balls
- Grapes (halve for young kids)
- Mango cubes
- Nectarine slices
- Orange sections
- Peach slices
- Pear slices
- Pineapple chunks
- Raspberries
- Strawberries
- Tangerine sections

HELPFUL FREEZING TIPS

■ Always freeze fruit in containers or bags that are specifically designed for freezer storage. Rigid airtight plastic containers and zip-lock freezer bags work well. Don't use plastic wrap or standard food storage bags—they aren't thick enough to keep out moisture.

■ Before freezing grapes or berries, wash them gently and drain well. Blot with paper towels to remove any excess moisture. For snacking purposes, it's best to loosely pack the berries for easy-to-retrieve snack-sized handfuls. Place them on a tray in a single layer and freeze for about an hour. Transfer the fruit to a proper storage bag or container and return to the freezer.

■ Like berries, before you freeze chunks of pineapple or slices of juicy fruits like apples, peaches, and apricots, pat some of the excess moisture with paper towels. Freeze as described in the previous entry.

■ Certain fruits like apples, peaches, and pears begin to turn brown after they are cut. You can help prevent them from browning by dipping the freshly cut slices in a solution of 2 cups water and 1 tablespoon lemon juice. Drain well before freezing.

■ Before freezing, label the container with the contents and the date. When properly stored, fruit can last up to a year in the freezer.

Really Raspberry Sorbet

Lemon juice and zest enhance the flavor of the fresh raspberries in this easy-to-make version of a classic frozen treat.

Yield: 2 servings

. . . .

2 cups tightly packed fresh raspberries

1/2 cup raspberry jam

1/2 teaspoon fresh lemon juice

3 teaspoons fresh lemon zest

1. Place the raspberries and jam in a blender or food processor and blend until smooth. Pour the mixture through a sieve or strainer to remove the seeds.

2. Add the lemon juice and zest to the raspberry mixture and stir until well blended.

3. Pour the mixture into a shallow freezer-safe bowl, cover, and place in the freezer until firm.

4. With an ice cream scoop or spoon, scoop the frozen sorbet into a bowl and serve.

CHANGE IT UP . . .

- For individual mini servings, freeze the raspberry mixture in ice cube trays.

- Instead of strawberries, use other jams and fruits, like blueberries and raspberries.

Confetti Popcorn Balls

You can make these fun-to-eat popcorn balls any size you want.
They make perfect lunchbox treats or take-along snacks.
You can air-pop the popcorn yourself, or use bagged popcorn
(which we actually prefer because of its crispness).

Yield: 40 to 45 balls
(1 1/2 inches)
• • • • • • • •
10 cups popped popcorn

1/3 cup dry roasted
sunflower seeds

1/3 cup dry roasted
pumpkin seeds

1/4 cup raisins

1/4 cup dried cranberries

1/4 cup chopped dates

1 cup date sugar

1/2 cup brown rice syrup

1/2 cup water

1/2 teaspoon sea salt
(optional)

1. Line a baking sheet with waxed paper and set aside.

2. Place the popcorn, sunflower seeds, pumpkin seeds, raisins, cranberries, and dates in a large bowl and mix well. Set aside.

3. Place the date sugar, rice syrup, water, and salt (if using) in a small pot over medium-low heat. Stirring slowly but constantly, warm the mixture for 4 to 5 minutes or until it becomes thick and goopy, like caramel.

4. Pour the hot mixture over the popcorn while stirring the ingredients with a wooden spoon until well coated. Allow to cool for about a minute, then dump the popcorn onto the wax paper-lined baking sheet to continue cooling.

5. While the popcorn mixture is still fairly hot but cool enough to handle, scoop up small handfuls and form into 1 1/2 - inch balls. Put a little oil on your hands to prevent the mixture from sticking to them. Work quickly before the mixture cools and becomes too firm to shape.

6. Arrange the popcorn balls on waxed paper to finish cooling. Store in an airtight container (make sure they are completely cool first) up to five days.

CHANGE IT UP . . .

• Instead of chopped dates, try other dried unsulfured fruit like pineapple, mango, blueberries, and apples.

• Toss in a small handful of sesame seeds for even more flavor and crunch.

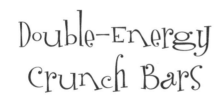
Double-Energy Crunch Bars

These sweet, chewy bars are a perfect on-the-go snack.

1. Lightly oil a 16-x-11-inch baking sheet/pan and set aside.

2. Place the sunflower seeds, sesame seeds, raisins, and coconut in a large bowl and mix well.

3. Heat the brown rice syrup in a large pot over medium-low heat for about 20 seconds. Add the sunflower seed butter and agave. Continue to heat while gently stirring for 30 seconds or until the mixture is hot, smooth, and creamy. Remove from the heat.

4. Stir the vanilla into the hot mixture, then add the crispy rice cereal and seed/dried fruit mixture. Stir well with a large wooden spoon or spatula until all of the ingredients are well coated.

5. Empty the mixture onto the prepared baking pan and spread out evenly with a spatula. With oiled hands, firmly pat down the mixture to $1/2$-inch thickness.

6. Place the pan in the refrigerator about an hour or until the mixture is firm.

7. With a sharp knife, cut the mixture into 2-inch squares. Layer the squares in an airtight container (separate each layer with a sheet of waxed paper) and refrigerate up to a week or freeze up to two months.

Yield: 35 bars
(2-inch squares)

• • • • • • •

I cup dry roasted
sunflower seeds

$1/2$ cup toasted
sesame seeds

$1/2$ cup raisins

$1/2$ cup unsweetened
shredded coconut

$3/4$ cup brown rice syrup

$3/4$ cup toasted sunflower
seed butter

$1/4$ cup agave nectar

I teaspoon vanilla

4 cups crisped brown
rice cereal

CHANGE IT UP . . .

• Instead of (or in addition to) raisins, try other dried unsulfured fruit like pineapple, mango, blueberries, cranberries, and apples.

Sunny Granola Crunch

Kids of all ages love this granola, which makes a great party mix.
It can also be enjoyed as a breakfast cereal with a splash of
rice milk and some fresh fruit.

Yield: About 8 cups

• • • • • • •

5 cups rolled oats

2 cups unsweetened shredded coconut

I cup raw sunflower seeds

$^1/_4$ cup raw sesame seeds

$^1/_2$ cup raisins

I tablespoon ground cinnamon

$^2/_3$ cup sunflower oil

$^1/_2$ cup honey

I tablespoon vanilla

1. Preheat the oven to 350°F.

2. Place the oats, coconut, sunflower seeds, sesame seeds, raisins, and cinnamon in a large bowl and stir until well mixed. Set aside.

3. Heat the oil and honey in a small saucepan over medium heat for about a minute or until the mixture is well blended. Remove from the heat, add the vanilla, and stir well.

4. Pour the honey mixture over the oat mixture and stir until well coated.

5. Spread the mixture on an unoiled baking sheet and bake for 7 or 8 minutes. Stir the mixture with a butter knife or spatula, then bake another 6 to 8 minutes or until browned and crisp.

6. Cool the granola completely before transferring to an airtight container or plastic zip-lock bag. Store in the pantry where it will keep up to a week. It will also keep in the freezer up to three months.

CHANGE IT UP . . .

• For added flavor and texture, add a cup or so of puffed corn or puffed rice to the granola after it has cooled.

• For maple-flavored granola, replace the honey with pure maple syrup.

No-Fail Trail Mix

*This fruit- and fiber-filled trail mix is the perfect on-the-go snack.
We try to always have some on hand for our kids
to enjoy at a moment's notice.*

Yield: 10 to 12 cups

· · · · · · ·

4 cups oat "O's" cereal
or organic corn flakes

2 cups raisins

2 cups dry roasted
sunflower seeds

2 cups dry roasted
pumpkin seeds

2 cups unsweetened
shredded coconut
(optional)

1. Place all of the ingredients in a large bowl and stir well.

2. Transfer to an airtight container or plastic zip-lock bag.

3. Store in the pantry where it will keep for about a week.

CHANGE IT UP . . .

- Add a cup of air-popped popcorn to the mix for added fiber.

- Instead of raisins, use any dried unsulfured fruit.

- If soy is not an issue, add a cup of unsweetened carob chips.

Marinated Figs

*Whether fresh or dried, plain or marinated, figs are a wonderfully
healthy snack. Fresh figs are very delicate and highly perishable,
while dried varieties can keep for months. When buying fresh figs,
select those that are plump and firm with a rich deep color.*

Yield: 16 figs

· · · · · · ·

16 figs, fresh or dried

1 1/2 cups apple juice

2 tablespoons lemon juice

1 tablespoon cinnamon

1. Place the figs and apple juice in a small saucepan and bring to
   a boil over medium-high heat. Reduce the heat to low and
   simmer for 1 minute. Remove from the heat.

2. Add the lemon juice to the fig mixture, then transfer to a
   medium bowl.

3. Cover and marinate in the refrigerator at least 8 hours.

4. Serve chilled or at room temperature.

Cinnamon Peaches

Yield: 2 servings

- 2 large ripe peaches, sliced
- $1/2$ cup water
- 1 tablespoon lemon juice
- 1 tablespoon pure maple syrup
- 1 teaspoon ground cinnamon
- 1 teaspoon ground ginger
- 2 tablespoons raisins

Adding a scoop of frozen Vanilla Rice Dream to this snack makes it extra special.

1. Preheat the oven to 350°F.

2. Place the peach slices in a small unoiled baking dish and set aside.

3. Whisk together the water, lemon juice, maple syrup, cinnamon, and ginger in a small bowl. Add the raisins, stir well, then pour over the peaches.

4. Bake uncovered for 15 minutes or until the peaches are soft.

5. Serve warm or refrigerate and serve cold.

Homestyle Baked Apples

Yield: 2 baked apples

- 2 large Rome or Cortland apples
- $1/4$ cup dark or golden raisins
- 1 teaspoon ground cinnamon

These sugar-free baked apples are naturally sweet. If tree nuts are not an issue, try adding some chopped pecans or walnuts.

1. Preheat the oven to 350°F. Toss the raisins with the cinnamon and set aside.

2. Core each apple. To help prevent the skins from bursting as they bake, remove about an inch of peel from the top of each apple, and then cut a line around the middle with a paring knife.

3. Place the apples in a small unoiled baking dish, and fill the cored centers with the raisins. Cover the bottom of the baking dish with about $1/2$ inch water.

4. Basting occasionally with the pan liquid, bake the apples uncovered for 45 to 50 minutes or until tender (not mushy) when pierced with a fork.

5. Serve warm, at room temperature, or refrigerate and serve chilled.

6

Savory Snack-Time Favorites

When people first think of snacks, images of cookies, muffins and other sweet treats often come to mind. In this chapter, we present a different side to snacks—a savory side.

Kicking off this chapter, we have spotlighted everyone's favorite vegetable—the potato. Seriously, do you know any kid who doesn't like French fries? Our oven-baked recipe for sweet potato fries comes with a variation for the classic version, and both are sure to please. There are also recipes for mashed potato patties, crisp potato skins, and an easy-to-prepare potato salad. Be sure to try the Rainbow Veggie Tater Tots. Shredded carrots and zucchini add a spark of color and nutritional goodness in this fun variation of classic "tots."

There are few foods that kids enjoy more than pizza. And just because your child may be gluten intolerant or allergic to wheat, dairy, or soy,

there is no reason he or she has to give up this snack favorite. To help, we have included an allergen-free/gluten-free Perfect Pizza Crust recipe and a tomato-based Quick 'n Easy Pizza Sauce to serve as a great pizza foundation. Then check out the "Have a Pizza Party" inset beginning on page 96 for an incredible assortment of suggested toppings—including some terrific cheeses.

Rounding out the chapter are recipes for mini burgers, sliders, and snack bites. You will find legume- and/or vegetable-based pleasers like Pinto Power Patties, Little Lentil Snackers, and Mini Veggie Burgers to mention a few. All of these snacks can be eaten as is, or shaped into "meat"balls and served with pasta.

No matter which snacks you choose, you can feel good in knowing that they are healthy and hearty. They will satisfy your kids in a delicious way.

Corny Corn Cakes

Corn cakes are a wonderful alternative to potato pancakes.
Serve them alone or topped with salsa, applesauce, or maple syrup.
Or spread some sunflower seed butter and jelly between
two cakes for a fun snack.

Yield: About 10 cakes
(3-inch rounds)
. . . .

1 cup cornmeal

$1/4$ cup brown rice flour

$1/4$ cup potato starch flour

1 cup cooked corn kernels

1 cup rice milk

3 tablespoons extra-virgin
olive oil, divided

1. Combine the cornmeal, brown rice flour, and potato starch flour in a large bowl. Add the corn kernels and stir until well distributed.

2. Add the rice milk and 1 tablespoon of the olive oil to the cornmeal mixture and stir to form a well-blended, somewhat thick batter. Set aside.

3. Heat the remaining oil in a medium skillet or griddle over medium heat.

4. Drop 2 heaping tablespoons of batter onto the skillet for each cake. Cook about 1 minute on each side or until browned and crisp.

5. Serve warm or at room temperature.

Sweet Potato Fries

Kids and adults alike love these sweet, colorful
oven-baked fries.

Yield: 4 to 6 servings
. . . .

2 pounds sweet potatoes
or yams

3 tablespoons extra-virgin
olive oil

1 tablespoon honey

1 teaspoon cinnamon

1. Preheat the oven to 350°F. Lightly oil a baking sheet and set aside.

2. Peel the potatoes and cut into $1/2$-inch-thick strips.

3. Place the strips in a large bowl. Add the oil, honey, and cinnamon, and toss until the strips are well coated.

4. Arrange the strips in a single layer on the prepared baking sheet.

5. Bake for 15 to 20 minutes or until crisp and brown.

6. Serve hot, warm or at room temperature.

CHANGE IT UP . . .

• For classic French fries, substitute white potatoes for the sweet, omit the honey, and use garlic salt instead of cinnamon. You can also leave these potatoes unpeeled.

Patty's Potato Patties

Whether these bite-sized oven-baked treats are served hot or cold, our kids never seem to get enough of them. They enjoy them plain or dipped in ketchup,

1. Preheat the over to 350°F. Lightly oil a baking sheet and set aside.

2. Boil the potatoes in a pot of water for 20 minutes or until fork tender. Remove and set aside until cool enough to handle.

3. Cut the cooled potatoes into cubes and place in a blender or food processor along with the remaining ingredients. Blend for about 2 minutes or until smooth and thick.

4. Form heaping tablespoons of the mixture into 3-inch patties and arrange on the prepared baking sheet.

5. Bake 18 to 20 minutes or until golden brown. Serve hot, warm, or at room temperature.

Yield: About 12 patties (3-inch rounds)

• • • • • • •

2 pounds red potatoes, unpeeled

1 medium yellow onion, finely chopped

4 tablespoons brown rice flour

3 tablespoons chopped parsley

2 tablespoons water

$\frac{1}{2}$ teaspoon garlic powder

1 teaspoon sea salt

Oven-Crisped Baked Potato Skins

Kids love these tasty potato skins,
especially when they're crisp and hot from the oven.

Yield: 16 potato skins

• • • • • • • •

4 medium baking potatoes

Olive oil
cooking spray

1 teaspoon garlic powder

Sea salt to taste

$1/4$ cup finely chopped
scallions (optional)

1. Preheat the oven to 450°F.

2. Pierce the potatoes in several places with the tines of a fork or the tip of a small knife, then lightly coat the skins with cooking spray.

3. Bake on the center rack of the oven for 40 to 45 minutes or until fork tender.

4. When cool enough to handle, quarter each potato lengthwise into wedges. With a spoon, carefully remove most of the flesh, leaving about $1/4$-inch on the skins.

5. Lightly coat the wedges with cooking spray, and sprinkle with garlic powder and sea salt. Arrange on a baking sheet and return to the oven.

6. Bake the skins for 5 minutes, turn them over, then bake another 5 minutes or until hot and crisp.

7. Serve as is or garnish with chopped scallions.

CHANGE IT UP . . .

• For added flavor and interest, top the crisp skins with a spoonful of your child's favorite dip or salsa. Mummy's Yummy Hummus (page 42), Festive Fiesta Salsa (page 34), and Chunky Black Bean Dip (page 35), are just a few of the many fantastic choices from Chapter 3.

EZ Potato Salad

When your kids are looking for a satisfying snack,
this tasty potato salad is a good choice.
Not only is it easy to make, you can even use leftover potatoes!

1. Boil the potatoes until fork tender. When cool enough to handle, peel off the skin with your fingers (or leave it on), and dice the potatoes into small, bite-sized pieces. Place in a medium mixing bowl.

2. Add all of the remaining ingredients and stir gently until well combined.

3. Serve warm or refrigerate and serve chilled.

CHANGE IT UP . . .

- For added flavor and crunch, toss some chopped pickles or scallions into the salad.

- Instead of Vegenaise, try one of the Dreamy Creamy Mayonnaise recipes on pages 38 and 39.

Yield: 2 cups

2 medium-sized new potatoes

2 tablespoons soy-free Vegenaise

1 tablespoon diced celery

1 tablespoon diced bell pepper

1 teaspoon white wine or apple cider vinegar

1 teaspoon Dijon-style mustard

$\frac{1}{4}$ teaspoon sea salt, or to taste

$\frac{1}{8}$ teaspoon garlic powder

NUTRITIONAL YEAST

Not to be confused with brewer's yeast, torula yeast, dry active yeast, or fresh cake yeast, nutritional yeast is a food supplement that is very rich in protein and B vitamins. It comes in thin golden flakes that add a rich, flavorful, slightly cheesy taste to many foods, including soups, spreads, veggie burgers, pizza, and even popcorn! Start with a small amount—a teaspoon or so—then add more to taste.

HAVE A PIZZA PARTY!

There are few foods that kids enjoy more than pizza—it's delicious, fun to eat, and lends itself to lots of flavorful toppings. And just because your child is gluten intolerant or has an allergy to wheat, soy, or dairy, it doesn't mean he or she has to give up this classic food favorite. As you can see, there are many ingredient options for creating perfectly delicious allergen-free pizzas!

First, the foundation of any pizza is the crust. With the growing number of commercial bread products that are gluten- and allergen-free, items like pita rounds and bagels, as well as corn or rice tortillas can make great pizza crusts. A number of manufacturers like Bob's Red Mill and Authentic Foods carry pizza crust mixes that are gluten-free, dairy-free, and can be made without eggs. If you want to try your hand at making your own crust from scratch, be sure to check out our Perfect Pizza Crust (page 98). Also be aware that there are lots of crust recipes—often shared by parents of kids with food allergies—on the Internet.

A layer of rich tomato-based sauce traditionally covers the crust. Although there are many commercial sauces you can choose, we hope you try our Quick 'n Easy Pizza Sauce (page 99)—it's a family recipe created by our Grandmother Giovanna, who came from a province in Tuscany. Of course, you can skip the tomato sauce altogether and use basil pesto (nut free) or even a simple brushing of olive oil.

Another classic pizza ingredient is cheese—specifically mozzarella and Parmesan varieties. For kids with a dairy allergy, cheese has always been the most difficult ingredient to replace. A number of dairy-free cheeses are on the market, but finding one that is similar to dairy varieties has been challenging. We recently discovered Daiya brand vegan mozzarella and found it to be pretty close in taste, texture, and melting capabilities (it's deliciously stretchy and gooey). Your kids will love it. And although we have yet to find a perfect substitute for Parmesan cheese, a number of decent vegan varieties are available. We have also found that a sprinkling of nutritional yeast flakes offers a rich, slightly cheesy flavor that resembles the taste of Parmesan.

When it comes to toppings, there is no shortage of ingredients thanks to the wide variety of fresh vegetables, legumes, herbs, and spices that are available. Here are some of our favorites:

- Artichoke hearts
- Asparagus tips
- Avocados
- Basil
- Bell peppers (all colors)
- Black beans
- Broccoli florets
- Capers
- Cherry tomatoes
- Chickpeas
- Eggplant
- Fennel
- Garlic
- Kale
- Mushrooms
- Olives
- Onions
- Oregano
- Rosemary
- Scallions
- Spinach
- Sun-dried tomatoes
- Tomatoes
- Zucchini

Along with our kids, over the years we have created some really sensational allergen-free pizzas with delicious ingredient combinations— some simple, others more complex. One thing we have learned is that when it comes to toppings, less is usually more. Too many flavors tend to compete with one another, so we try to limit toppings (not including herbs and spices) to two or three.

- ❑ Pesto with sliced tomatoes.
- ❑ Sautéed sliced mushrooms and caramelized onions.
- ❑ Sliced tomato, chopped red onion, and fresh basil.
- ❑ Sun-dried tomatoes, marinated artichoke hearts, and black olives.
- ❑ Black beans, diced tomatoes, and chopped scallions.
- ❑ Grilled eggplant, yellow bell pepper, and sliced red onion.
- ❑ Thinly sliced potatoes, chopped onions, and rosemary.
- ❑ Artichoke hearts, capers, and garlic.

Below, we have shared a few of our favorites topping combinations with you. Hope you enjoy trying them out with your kids, as well as creating specialty pizzas of your own.

Top any of the following combinations with vegan mozzarella, Parmesan, cheddar, and/or a sprinkling of nutritional yeast flakes. Also season as desired with herbs and spices, including salt and pepper:

- ❑ Grilled zucchini slices, sliced onions, and sautéed mushrooms.
- ❑ Broccoli florets, roasted bell pepper, and roasted garlic.
- ❑ Salsa, corn kernels, kidney beans, and fresh cilantro.
- ❑ Avocado, sun-dried tomatoes, and black olives.
- ❑ Steamed asparagus tips, roasted red bell pepper, and fresh basil.
- ❑ Sautéed kale, halved cherry tomatoes, and chopped scallions.
- ❑ Herb combo (basil, oregano, and rosemary), black olives, and olive oil.

FAVORITE NO-BAKE PIZZAS

■ Spread a thick layer of Mummy's Yummy Hummus (page 42) on a lightly toasted corn tortilla. Top with some chopped fresh tomatoes, chopped scallion, corn kernels, and fresh cilantro.

■ Toss shredded lettuce, grated carrots, halved cherry tomatoes, and sliced black olives with a vinaigrette dressing. Place over a prebaked pizza crust for a "salad pizza."

Perfect Pizza Crust

*Mama Mia! This allergen-free/gluten-free dough
makes a great pizza crust.*

Yield: 4 thin crusts
(8-inch rounds)

• • • • • • •

2¼ teaspoons active dry
yeast (¼-ounce packet)

1½ cups warm
(not hot) water

1 teaspoon honey

2 tablespoons olive oil

1½ teaspoons dried
Italian seasoning blend

1 teaspoon sea salt

2 cups brown rice flour

1½ cups tapioca flour

1. Dissolve the yeast in a cup or small bowl with ½ cup of the warm water and the honey. The mixture should bubble up and foam within a minute or so. If it doesn't, the yeast is not good. Discard it and start over with fresh yeast.

2. Transfer the dissolved yeast to a large mixing bowl along with the remaining warm water, the oil, Italian seasoning blend, and salt. Stir well with a wooden spoon.

3. Add 1 cup of the brown rice flour to the bowl and stir well. Continue to stir while adding the remaining brown rice flour and tapioca flour. When the dough becomes too stiff to stir and starts pulling away from the sides of the bowl, it's time to knead.

4. Turn the dough (it will be sticky) onto a clean surface that has been sprinkled with rice flour. Knead the dough for 4 or 5 minutes, while continuing to sprinkle with flour, until it is smooth and no longer sticky.

5. Place the dough in a large, well-oiled bowl, then turn it over so the top is coated with oil—coating the dough will keep it from drying out. (You can use the same bowl you used to mix the ingredients, and you don't have to clean it first.) Cover the bowl with a clean damp dishtowel or plastic wrap. Place in a warm spot for about 30 minutes or until the dough doubles in bulk.

6. Preheat the oven to 400°F. Lightly oil a baking sheet and set aside.

7. Punch down the risen dough, fold it over a few times, then let rest a minute.

8. Divide the dough into 4 equal pieces and shape into balls.

9. Place each ball between sheets of waxed paper and roll out to 10-inch circles about ⅛ inch thick. Pinch the edges with your fingers to create a slightly raised border.

10. Place the rounds on the prepared baking sheet and bake for 8 to 10 minutes. Remove from the oven, add the desired toppings, then return to the oven for an additional 15 to 20 minutes or until the bottom of the crust is browned.

11. You can also prebake the crusts for 15 to 20 minutes, freeze them, and finish baking (with toppings) at a later time. Just be sure to cool the crusts completely. Then wrap each crust in plastic wrap, place in a freezer-quality storage bag, and freeze up to two months.

CHANGE IT UP . . .

- For added crunch, sprinkle the oiled baking sheet with a handful of cornmeal before adding the dough. The cornmeal will bake into the bottom of the crusts, just like those made in a pizzeria!

- For dough that is a bit flaky and doesn't rise as much, use oat flour instead of the brown rice/tapioca flour combo.

- For more pizza crust ideas, see "Have a Pizza Party" on page 96.

Quick 'n Easy Pizza Sauce

*When fresh tomatoes and herbs weren't available,
our Grandma Giovanna made this quick and easy tomato sauce.
Perfect not only for pizza, but for pasta as well.*

1. Heat the oil in a large pot over medium-low heat. Add the onion and garlic, and sauté 5 to 8 minutes or until the onions begin to soften.

2. Add all of the remaining ingredients and stir well.

3. Increase the heat to medium-high and bring the sauce to a boil. Reduce the heat to low and simmer uncovered, stirring often, for at least 30 minutes or until the sauce reaches the desired thickness. (The longer it simmers, the thicker it will get and the less acidic it will taste.)

4. Use immediately or refrigerate in an airtight container up to a week. Freeze up to six months.

Yield: About 4 cups

3 tablespoons extra-virgin olive oil

1 medium yellow onion, diced

1 clove garlic, minced

29-ounce can tomato purée

28-ounce can crushed tomatoes

1 tablespoon honey

1 tablespoon dried Italian herb seasoning

1 tablespoon dried basil

$1/2$ teaspoon sea salt

JUST FOR FUN!

Kids love eating snacks that come in fun shapes. And nothing does the job better than cookie cutters, which come in about a zillion different shapes and sizes. They can transform everyday snacks into snack sensations!

★ Cut out slices of bread to make fun-shaped sandwiches.

♣ Cut rice or corn tortillas into special shapes before baking them into crisp chips to serve with dip.

🐘 Make raw crunchy vegetables—like jicama, large carrots, and yellow summer squash—more visually appealing to kids. After slicing the veggies into $1/8$-inch-thick circles, use cookie cutters (metal are best) to press out different shapes. And don't forget to use the scraps in a salad!

♥ Cut watermelon, cantaloupe, or honeydew into thick slices, then use cookie cutters to transform them into circles, flowers, or heart shapes. Serve the slices as they are or on popsicle sticks.

✖ With the help of a melon baller (not really a cookie cutter, but kind of close), you can create tiny snack-sized balls out of melons—always fun for kids. Use the leftover scraps to make smoothies or frozen fruit pops.

Burritos 2 Go

Yield: 4 burritos

• • • • • • •

15-ounce can black beans, rinsed and drained

$1/4$ cup salsa

2 scallions, chopped

4 brown rice tortillas (6-inch rounds)

2 tablespoons extra-virgin olive oil

Black beans add protein and fiber to these mini burritos.
To make them even "more mini," cut the filled burritos in half.

1. Place the beans, salsa, and scallions in a blender or food processor and blend for about 20 seconds or until the mixture is smooth.

2. Spread 2 heaping tablespoons of the bean mixture on each tortilla, roll up tightly, and set aside (seam side down).

3. Heat the oil in a skillet over medium heat.

4. Place the burritos in the skillet seam side down, and gently flatten a bit with a spatula. Cook for about 1 minute or until the filling is hot and the bottoms are slightly brown. Serve warm.

CHANGE IT UP . . .

● For added taste and crunch, stir $^1/_2$ cup cooked corn kernels into the filling mixture.

● Use pinto beans instead of black beans.

Falafel Mini Mounds

It's important to use soaked dried chickpeas for this recipe—cooked chickpeas contain too much liquid and the falafel won't hold its shape.

1. Preheat the oven to 400°F. Lightly oil a baking sheet and set aside.

2. Drain the soaked chickpeas well and transfer to a food processor along with all the remaining ingredients except the parsley and water.

3. Process the mixture about 1 minute or until it comes together and is fairly smooth. If it seems too dry, add a teaspoon of water at a time, but no more than 2 tablespoons. (Too much liquid will cause the mixture to fall apart as it bakes.) Add the parsley and stir until well distributed.

4. Shape the mixture into $1^1/_2$-inch balls and place on the prepared baking sheet.

5. Bake 10 to 12 minutes or until the bottoms are lightly browned. Serve warm.

Yield: About 18 mounds

● ● ● ● ● ● ●

1 cup dried chickpeas, soaked 24 hours

1 small yellow onion, finely chopped

1 small garlic clove, minced

1 tablespoon lemon juice

1 teaspoon lemon zest

1 teaspoon cumin seeds (optional)

$^1/_2$ teaspoon baking soda

1 teaspoon sea salt

$^1/_8$ teaspoon black pepper

1 tablespoon chopped fresh parsley

1–2 tablespoons water, if necessary

Chickpea-Pumpkin Sliders

Yield: 10 to 12 sliders

- - - - - - - -

1 cup cooked chickpeas, well drained

1 cup cooked lentils, well drained

1/4 cup pumpkin purée

$1/_4$ cup chickpea flour

$1/_2$ cup chopped onion

1 clove garlic, minced

1 teaspoon cumin

1 teaspoon dried cilantro

1 teaspoon curry powder (optional)

$1/_2$ teaspoon sea salt

1–2 tablespoons extra-virgin olive oil

They may be small, but these protein-rich mini burgers pack a satisfying punch. Serve them alone or on mini rice cakes . . . the perfect snack.

1. Place chickpeas, lentils, and pumpkin purée in a food processor or blender, and pulse until coarsely chopped.

2. Add all of the remaining ingredients except the oil, and continue to pulse another 10 seconds to form a very moist, somewhat chunky mixture.

3. Scoop up small handfuls of the mixture to form 2- to 3-inch patties about $1/_2$ inch thick.

4. Heat 1 tablespoon of the oil in a large skillet over medium heat.

5. Add the patties to the skillet and cook about 5 minutes on each side until crisp. (Add more oil as needed during cooking.)

6. Serve hot, warm, or at room temperature.

GIVE IT SOME ZING!

Serving a dip with the mini burgers and snack bites in this section, or adding a condiment, garnish, or topping can increase visual appeal while enhancing flavor and texture. Along with the salsas, dips, and spreads in Chapter 3, here are a few more suggested additions and accompaniments:

- Carrot curls
- Cheese (soy/dairy free)
- Chopped bell peppers
- Chopped scallions
- Chopped tomatoes
- Cucumber slices
- Guacamole
- Hot sauce
- Hummus
- Ketchup

Itty Bitty Burgers

Talk about having it all! Not only do these mini burgers contain veggies, beans, and grains, they also taste great!

1. Preheat the oven to 350°F. Lightly oil a baking sheet and set aside.

2. Place the onion in a food processor and pulse until finely chopped. Transfer to a medium mixing bowl.

3. Cut the carrots into chunks, place in the food processor, and pulse until finely chopped. Add to the onions, along with all of the remaining ingredients except the flour, and mix well.

4. Add the flour to the mixture and stir well.

5. Scoop up small handfuls of the mixture to form 2- to 3-inch patties about $1/2$ inch thick.

6. Place the patties on the prepared baking sheet. Bake for 13 to 15 minutes, then gently turn over with a spatula and cook an additional 10 minutes or until slightly browned and crisp.

7. Serve hot, warm, or at room temperature.

Yield: 10 to 12 mini burgers

• • • • • • • •

1 medium yellow onion

2 medium carrots

15-ounce can black beans, rinsed and drained

1 cup cooked quinoa

$1/2$ cup mashed sweet potato (1 small)

1 clove garlic, minced

1 tablespoon nutritional yeast (optional)

1 teaspoon sea salt

$1/2$ tablespoon chopped fresh parsley

$1/4$ cup brown rice flour

ZING! ZING!

- Lettuce leaves
- Mushroom slices (raw/cooked)
- Mustard
- Olive slices
- Pesto (nut-free)
- Pickle slices
- Pickle relish
- Pizza sauce
- Roasted bell pepper strips
- Salsa
- Shredded cabbage
- Spinach
- Sprouts
- Sunflower seed butter
- Vegenaise (soy free)
- Zucchini slices

Little Lentil Snackers

We usually spear these snack-sized balls with toothpicks
and serve them with ketchup or other tomato-based sauce or dip.

Yield: About 30 snackers

$2\frac{1}{2}$ cups cooked lentils

2 tablespoons oat flour

$\frac{1}{4}$ cup chunky salsa

1 clove garlic, minced

1 tablespoon
nutritional yeast

1 teaspoon curry powder

1 teaspoon sea salt

1 tablespoon olive oil

1. Preheat the oven to 350°F. Lightly oil a baking sheet and set aside.

2. Place the lentils, salsa, oat flour, garlic, and nutritional yeast in a blender or food processor. Pulse about 15 seconds or until the mixture is fairly smooth. Transfer to a large mixing bowl.

3. Stir the curry powder and salt into the lentil mixture. Add the oil and mix well.

4. Form the mixture into $1\frac{1}{2}$-inch balls and arrange on the prepared baking sheet.

5. Bake for 25 to 30 minutes or until firm and browned.

6. Serve warm or at room temperature.

Black Bean Bites

Nutrient-rich spinach adds mild flavor to the black beans in these snack-sized mini burgers.

Yield: 10 to 12 mini burgers

• • • • • • • •

15-ouce can black beans; rinsed and drained

1 medium yellow onion, quartered

1 cup chopped cooked spinach

$1/2$ cup rolled oats

$1/4$ teaspoon sea salt

3 tablespoons water, if necessary

1–2 tablespoons extra-virgin olive oil

1. Place the beans, onion, spinach, and oats in food processor and pulse until well combined but slightly chunky. If the mixture seems too dry, add the water 1 tablespoon at a time until it is moist enough to hold together.

2. Scoop up small handfuls of the mixture to form 2- to 3-inch patties about $1/2$ inch thick.

3. Heat 1 tablespoon of the oil in a large skillet over medium heat.

4. Add the patties to the skillet and cook about 5 minutes on each side or until browned and crisp. (Add more oil as needed during cooking.)

5. Serve hot, warm, or at room temperature.

Pinto Power Patties

Packed with protein and fiber, tasty pinto beans are the featured ingredient in these delicious burgers.

Yield: 10 to 12 mini patties

• • • • • • • •

1 tablespoon extra-virgin olive oil

1 small yellow onion, diced

$\frac{1}{2}$ cup chopped mushrooms

2 cups cooked pinto beans, rinsed and drained

$\frac{1}{2}$ cup toasted sunflower seeds

1 garlic clove, minced

1 teaspoon ground cumin

$\frac{1}{4}$ teaspoon ginger (optional)

$\frac{1}{4}$ cup brown rice flour

$\frac{1}{2}$ teaspoon sea salt

1. Preheat the oven to 350°F. Lightly oil a baking sheet and set aside.

2. Heat the olive oil in a medium skillet over medium heat. Add the onion and mushrooms, and sauté 3 to 5 minutes or until the onions begin to soften and the mushrooms are slightly wilted. Remove from the heat and let cool a few minutes.

3. Place the pinto beans in a food process and blend for 1 minute or until smooth. Add the rice flour, sunflower seeds, garlic, cumin, ginger (if using), and the sautéed onion-mushroom mixture. Pulse until the mixture is well blended and slightly chunky. Add the sea salt and stir well.

4. Scoop up small handfuls of the mixture to form 2- to 3-inch patties about $\frac{1}{2}$ inch thick.

5. Place the patties on the prepared baking sheet. Bake about 10 minutes on each side or until browned and crisp.

6. Serve hot, warm, or at room temperature.

SUNFLOWER POWER

Many people who are allergic to peanuts and tree nuts have found that sunflower seeds—with their mild nutty taste and firm, yet tender texture—make an excellent substitute. Packed with protein, fiber, B vitamins, and important minerals like calcium and iron, sunflower seeds are delicious raw or toasted. And sunflower seed butter is thick and creamy and can be used like peanut butter and nut butters. The seeds have a high oil content (they are a major source of polyunsaturated oil), which means they can become rancid easily. We find that storing them in an airtight container in the freezer is best. It does not affect their taste or texture, and they will keep for many months.

Mini Veggie Burgers

A kid-pleasing snack favorite!

1. Preheat the oven to 350°F. Lightly oil a baking sheet and set aside.

2. Place the sunflower seeds in a food processor and grind to a coarse meal. Set aside.

3. Heat the oil in a large skillet over medium heat. Add the onion, carrot, and celery seeds, and sauté for 5 minutes or until the carrot is soft. Remove from the heat and let cool a few minutes.

4. Place the flour, nutritional yeast flakes (if using), tomato paste, and salt in a large mixing bowl. Add the lentils, brown rice, garlic, sautéed onion-carrot mixture, and ground sunflower seeds. Stir until well mixed.

5. Scoop up small handfuls of the mixture to form 2- to 3-inch patties about $\frac{1}{2}$ inch thick.

6. Place the patties on the prepared baking sheet and bake for 10 minutes on each side or until browned and firm.

7. Serve hot, warm, or at room temperature.

Yield: 10 to 12 mini burgers

• • • • • • • •

$\frac{1}{2}$ cup toasted sunflower seeds

1 $\frac{1}{2}$ tablespoons olive oil

$\frac{1}{2}$ cup diced onion

1 large carrot, peeled and grated

$\frac{1}{4}$ teaspoon celery seeds

$\frac{1}{2}$ cup oat flour

2 tablespoons nutritional yeast (optional)

2 tablespoons tomato paste or sauce

$\frac{1}{2}$ teaspoon sea salt, or to taste

2 cups cooked lentils, well drained

$\frac{1}{2}$ cup cooked brown rice or amaranth

1 clove garlic, minced

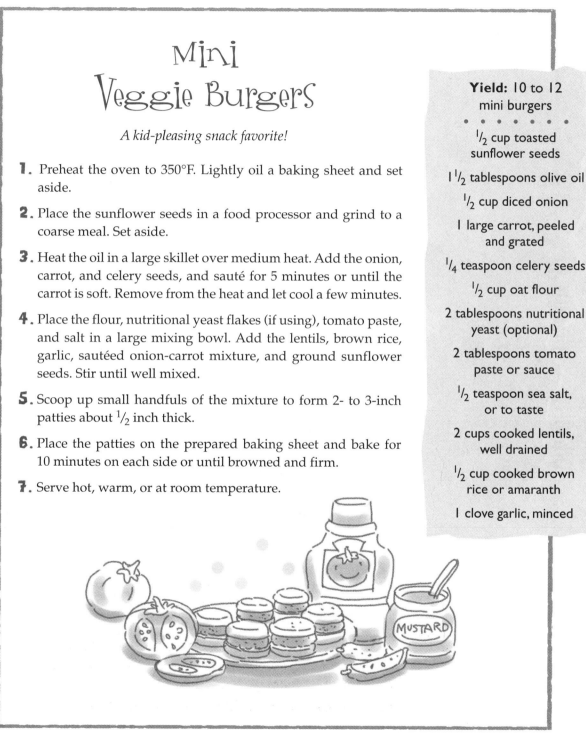

Rainbow Veggie Tater Tots

*Snacking on traditional tater tots is always fun for kids.
In this oven-baked variation, colorful vegetables are added
to boost nutritional value and add a rainbow of color.
Your kids are gonna love 'em!*

Yield: About 24 tots

• • • • • • • •

3 cups grated potatoes

$^1/_2$ cup grated carrots

$^1/_2$ cup grated zucchini

$^1/_3$ cup oat flour

1 teaspoon sea salt

$^1/_2$ teaspoon black pepper

1 tablespoon extra-virgin
olive oil

1. Preheat the oven to 375°F. Oil a baking sheet and set aside.

2. Scoop up handfuls of the grated potatoes and squeeze to remove as much liquid as possible. Place in a large mixing bowl.

3. Squeeze the liquid from the grated carrots and the zucchini, then add to the potatoes.

4. Add the flour, salt, pepper, and oil to the grated vegetables and stir well.

5. Shape heaping tablespoons of the mixture into 1-inch mounds and place on the prepared baking sheet.

6. Bake the tots for 15 minutes or until they begin to brown on the bottom. Turn over with a spatula and continue to bake another 10 to 15 minutes or until crisp and golden brown.

7. Serve warm or at room temperature, either plain or alongside ketchup for dipping.

CHANGE IT UP . . .

- Use other colorful veggies for this recipe. Shredded green, orange, and/or red bell peppers are good choices, as are ruby red beets.

- For added flavor, stir $^1/_2$ cup finely grated onion into the mixture.

- To make these tots with potatoes only, use 4 cups shredded potatoes. You can use either white potatoes or sweet potatoes (or a mixture of both).

- Instead of oat flour, use chickpea or brown rice flour.

7

Smoothies, Spritzers, and Juice Drinks

There are many times when a delicious beverage is all a kid needs to satisfy the desire for a snack. And if that beverage is nutritious and made with fresh ingredients, you can feel good about serving it. This chapter is filled with bright, fruity, healthful drinks—liquid refreshers ranging from homemade lemonade and herbal tea coolers to sparkling juice drinks and thick, rich smoothies.

Although smoothies started out decades ago as a West Coast fad, they are definitely here to stay. In addition to making great snacks, they can be enjoyed as light breakfasts, desserts, or accompaniments to any meal. The foundation of any smoothie is fruit or fruit juice that is blended with ice, which adds thickness. But there are many more ingredients that can transform a simple smoothie into a luscious beverage with added flavor and nutrition.

The inset on page 114, "Fresh and Fruity— Create-a-Smoothie," presents a partial (but extensive) list of recommended ingredients for making delicious drinks that are rich sources of vitamins, minerals, and other healthful nutrients.

Although soy and dairy products are often used to flavor and thicken smoothies, the recipes in this chapter will show how non-allergenic products like fruit sorbet, sunflower seed butter, bananas, and even creamy avocadoes can produce the same delicious results.

So now it's time to take out the blender and wow your kids with some super smoothies, frosty slushies, and refreshing fruit juice sparklers and coolers. They are easy to make, fun to drink, and healthful—talk about a winning combination.

Very Berry Smoothie

Grape juice adds great color to this frosty drink.

Yield: 2 servings
(about 8 ounces each)

• • • • • •

1 1/2 cups raspberries,
blackberries,
and/or strawberries

1 cup grape juice

4–6 ice cubes

1. Place all the ingredients in a blender.

2. Blend on high speed about 1 minute or until the mixture is thick and the ice is well crushed.

3. Serve immediately.

Pineapple-Banana Smoothie

*Banana and pineapple are perfectly paired
in this classic smoothie.*

Yield: 2 servings
(about 8 ounces each)

• • • • • • •

1 cup rice milk

1 medium-sized ripe
banana, cut into
small chunks

1/2 cup crushed pineapple

1 tablespoon honey or
brown rice syrup

4–6 ice cubes

1. Place all the ingredients in a blender.

2. Blend on high speed about 1 minute or until the mixture is thick and the ice is well crushed.

3. Serve immediately.

FROZEN FRUIT OR ICE CUBES?

The foundation of any smoothie is fruit or fruit juice that is often thickened with ice. Instead of ice, you can use frozen fruit. Either buy fruit that is already frozen or freeze your own fresh varieties. Wash the fruit, dry it well, and then place it in a zip-lock freezer bag. This is an especially good idea for berries, which are not always in season and spoil quickly. Frozen, they can last for months!

Funky Monkey Smoothie

Carob powder gives this thick, rich drink the delicious flavor of chocolate.

1. Place the carob powder and 2 tablespoons of the rice milk in a cup or small bowl and stir until the carob is dissolved. Transfer to a blender and add the remaining ingredients.

2. Blend on high speed about 1 minute or until the mixture is smooth and the ice is crushed.

3. Serve immediately.

Yield: 3 servings
(about 8 ounces each)
• • • • • • •
1 tablespoon carob powder

2 cups rice milk

2 medium-sized ripe bananas, cut into small chunks

3 tablespoons honey or brown rice syrup

1 teaspoon vanilla

4–6 ice cubes

Green Blueberry Smoothie

This delicious smoothie has the added nutritional benefit of spinach—and kids won't even realize it!

1. Place all the ingredients in a blender.

2. Blend on high speed about 1 minute or until the mixture is smooth and the ice is well crushed.

3. Serve immediately.

Yield: 2 servings
(about 8 ounces each)
• • • • • • •
2 cups water

2 cups fresh blueberries

1 medium-sized ripe banana, cut into small chunks

1 cup fresh spinach

2 tablespoons maple syrup

4–6 ice cubes

Rockin' Raspberry Smoothie

Yield: 2 servings
(about 8 ounces each)
. . . .
1 ripe avocado, peeled
cut into chunks

³/₄ cup frozen raspberries

³/₄ cup raspberry juice

³/₄ cup orange juice

Along with adding rich creaminess to this "very raspberry" smoothie, nutrient-rich avocado offers amazing health benefits.

1. Place all the ingredients in a blender.
2. Blend on high speed about 1 minute or until the mixture is smooth and creamy.
3. Serve immediately.

Totally Tropical Smoothie

Yield: 3 servings
(about 8 ounces each)
. . . .
2 medium-sized ripe
bananas, cut into
small chunks

2 cups diced mango

¹/₂ cup crushed pineapple

¹/₄ cup unsweetened
flaked coconut

1 tablespoon
raspberry jam

4–6 ice cubes

Mmmm . . . this yummy smoothie made with tropical fruit favorites is always a hit!

1. Place all the ingredients in a blender.
2. Blend on high speed about 1 minute or until the mixture is smooth and the ice is well crushed.
3. Serve immediately.

Carrot-Mango Smoothie

This smoothie is not only frosty and delicious, it's also packed with vitamins B, C, and E.

1. Place all the ingredients in a blender.

2. Blend on high speed about 1 minute or until the mixture is smooth and the ice is well crushed.

3. Serve immediately.

Yield: 2 servings
(about 8 ounces each)

· · · · · · · ·

1 1/2 cups carrot juice

1 cup frozen mango
chunks

4–6 ice cubes

CHANGE IT UP . . .

- For a thicker drink, leave out the ice cubes.

Tutti-Frutti Smoothie

Although this smoothie is made with frozen fruit, you can use fresh as well—just be sure to add about six ice cubes in Step 2.

1. Place the fruit, rice milk, and vanilla in a blender and purée about 1 minute.

2. Add the honey and continue to blend another minute or until the mixture is thick and smooth.

3. Serve immediately.

Yield: 2 servings
(about 8 ounces each)

· · · · · · · ·

1 1/2 cups frozen fruit
(bananas, blueberries,
peaches, raspberries,
and/or strawberries)

1 cup rice milk

1/4 teaspoon vanilla

2 tablespoons honey

FRESH AND FRUITY CREATE-A-SMOOTHIE!

Smoothies are healthy, satisfying ways for kids of any age to enjoy their fruit. And you can whip one up in a matter of minutes. Although the foundation of a basic smoothie is fruit or fruit juice that is often thickened with ice, there are lots of ingredients (and ingredient combinations) that can turn a simple smoothie into a luscious drink with added flavor, richness, and nutritional value.

We've listed some of our favorite smoothie ingredients below. Have fun coming up with your own flavorful creations.

JUICES

• Apple	• Goji berry	• Orange	• Pomegranate
• Blueberry	• Grape	• Papaya	• Raspberry
• Carrot	• Grapefruit	• Peach	• Strawberry
• Cherry	• Kiwi	• Pear	• Watermelon
• Cranberry	• Mango	• Pineapple	

WHOLE FRUITS (PEELED/PITTED)

• Apricots	• Cantaloupes	• Mangoes	• Plums
• Bananas	• Grapes	• Papayas	• Raspberries
• Blackberries	• Honeydews	• Peaches	• Strawberries
• Blueberries	• Kiwis	• Pears	• Watermelon

THICKENERS

• Avocados	• Ice cubes	• Sunflower butter
• Bananas	• Sorbet	• Tahini

FLAVORFUL GOODIES

• Agave nectar	• Coconut flakes	• Goji berries	• Rice milk
• Brown rice syrup	• Coconut milk	• Honey	• Seed butters
• Carob powder	• Dates	• Lemon/lime juice	• Tea
• Cinnamon	• Ginger*	• Maple syrup	• Vanilla extract

* Fresh ginger is very strong. Start with just a little—a scant 1/4 teaspoon of grated ginger per 12-ounce drink—then adjust as desired.

Carob-Banana Smoothie

Bananas make this carob-flavored smoothie rich and creamy, while dates add a touch of sweetness.

1. Place all the ingredients in a blender.

2. Blend on high speed about 1 minute or until the mixture is smooth and the ice is well crushed.

3. Serve immediately.

Yield: 2 servings
(about 10 ounces each)
• • • • • • •
4 medium-sized ripe
bananas, cut into
small chunks

5 dates, chopped

3–4 tablespoons
carob powder

6–8 ice cubes

Green Tea and Goji Berry Smoothie

With a shape and texture that is similar to raisins, goji berries add a mild tangy flavor to this delicious smoothie.

1. Place the tea bags in a cup, cover with the boiling water, and steep for 3 minutes. Remove the tea bags and let the tea cool completely.

2. Transfer the cooled tea to a blender. Add the remaining ingredients and blend on high speed for 1 minute or until the mixture is smooth and the ice is well crushed.

3. Pour into glasses, garnish with a few goji berries, and serve immediately.

Yield: 2 servings
(about 8 ounces each)
• • • • • • •
2 decaffeinated
green tea bags

$\frac{1}{2}$ cup boiling water

2 large frozen
bananas, sliced

$\frac{1}{4}$ cup dried or fresh
goji berries, or $\frac{1}{4}$ cup
goji berry juice

2 tablespoons honey or
agave nectar

4–6 ice cubes

Honeydew-Kiwi Smoothie

Yield: 2 servings
(about 8 ounces each)
• • • • • • • •
2 cups cubed honeydew

1 1/2 cups cubed kiwi

1 tablespoon lime juice

1 tablespoon honey

1 teaspoon vanilla

6–8 ice cubes

*This sweet melon-flavored smoothie is light and refreshing—
perfect to serve on a hot day.*

1. Place all the ingredients in a blender.

2. Blend on high speed about 1 minute or until the mixture is
smooth and the ice is well crushed.

3. Serve immediately.

Caribbean Coco-Loco Smoothie

Yield: 2 servings
(about 8 ounces each)
• • • • • • • •
1 cup frozen mango
chunks

3/4 cup rice milk

1/2 cup coconut milk

1/2 cup pineapple or
pineapple-orange juice

1 teaspoon vanilla

4–6 ice cubes

A tropical delight!

1. Place all the ingredients in a blender.

2. Blend on high speed about 1 minute or until the mixture is
smooth and the ice is well crushed.

3. Serve immediately.

Papa's Papaya Smoothie

We usually serve this tropical island special with a wedge of fresh pineapple.

1. Place all the ingredients in a blender.

2. Blend on high speed about 1 minute or until the mixture is smooth and the ice is well crushed.

3. Serve immediately.

Yield: 3 servings (about 8 ounces each)

• • • • • • • •

2 cups chopped papaya

I medium-sized ripe banana, cut into small chunks

I cup pineapple juice

$^1/_2$ cup rice milk

I tablespoon honey

4–6 ice cubes

Peachy Granola Smoothie

Naturally sweet and juicy, the delicious peach is spotlighted in this luscious smoothie.

1. Place all ingredients a blender.

2. Blend on high speed about 1 minute or until the mixture is smooth and the ice is well crushed.

3. Serve immediately.

Yield: 2 servings (about 8 ounces each)

• • • • • • •

$^2/_3$ cup rice milk

I large ripe peach (about 6 ounces), cut into small chunks

$^1/_3$ cup granola (try the Sunny Granola Crunch on page 88)

$^1/_2$ teaspoon vanilla

4–6 ice cubes

California Sunshine Sparkler

Very light . . . very refreshing.

Yield: 2 servings
(about 8 ounces each)

• • • • • • • •

1 cup fresh or frozen
blueberries

1 cup seedless grapes

1 tablespoon brown rice
syrup or honey

1 cup sparkling water

1. Place the blueberries, grapes, and brown rice syrup in a blender, and blend on medium speed for 1 minute.

2. Add the sparkling water and stir on low speed for a few seconds.

3. Pour in glasses over ice and serve.

JUST FOR FUN!

There's nothing like a frosty ice pop to put a smile on any kid's face. Just fill popsicle molds with your kid's favorite juice or smoothie and pop in the freezer. You can also:

❧ Fill the molds with chunks of fruit before adding juice. We usually pack each individual mold with a variety of different fruit—crushed pineapple, blueberries, grapes, strawberries, etc.—which gives each pop a magnificent rainbow of colors. The pops are not only beautiful to look at but delicious as well.

❧ Fill the molds about halfway, freeze, and then fill the rest of the mold with juice of a contrasting color. This gives the pops a fun layered look and two different flavors. (You can also make three or even four layers.)

❧ Freeze the juice in ice cube trays to make fun-n-fruity ice cubes for cooling individual drinks or decorating party punch bowls. Dropping a piece of fruit, like a cherry, a raspberry, or a chunk of pineapple, into the individual cubes makes them even more fun and festive.

Apple-Ginger Spritz

The combination of Granny Smith apples and carrot juice gives this refreshing drink a sweet-tart taste, while the ginger adds a flavorful spark.

1. Place all the ingredients in a blender.

2. Blend on high speed about 30 seconds or until the mixture is smooth.

3. Pour in glasses over ice, garnish with a slice of green apple, and serve immediately.

CHANGE IT UP . . .

• For a sweeter drink, use a sweeter variety of apple, such as Delicious (red or golden), Fuji, or Gala.

Yield: 2 servings
(about 8 ounces each)
• • • • • • •
3 Granny Smith apples, peeled and cut into small chunks (about 2 cups)

1 cup carrot juice

$1/4$ teaspoon ground ginger

1 tablespoon lime juice

$1/2$ cup sparkling water

Banana Frosty Freeze

This drink is smooth, creamy, and super frosty!

1. Place all the ingredients in a blender.

2. Blend on high speed about 1 minute or until the mixture is smooth and the ice is well crushed.

3. Serve immediately.

Yield: 3 servings
(about 8 ounces each)
• • • • • • •
2 medium-sized ripe bananas, cut into small chunks

$1 1/2$ cups frozen peach slices

$1/2$ cup frozen orange juice concentrate

$1/2$ cup rice milk

1 teaspoon honey

4–6 ice cubes

Lemon Cooler

*There's nothing like the taste of homemade lemonade.
It's the perfect drink to serve with the chips and dips in Chapter 3!*

**Yield: 4 servings
(8 ounces each)**

• • • • • • •

²/₃ cup fresh lemon juice
(3 to 4 large lemons)

¹/₃ cup date sugar,
or to taste

3 cups cold water

1. Place the lemon juice and date sugar in a small bowl and stir until the sugar is dissolved.

2. Transfer the mixture to a pitcher, add the cold water, and stir well.

3. Serve as is or over ice.

CHANGE IT UP . . .

• For an added spark of flavor and to turn the lemonade a fun pink color, add ¹/₄ cup cranberry or raspberry juice.

• For a carbonated version, use sparkling water.

Spicy Chai Tea Cooler

*If your kids like the spicy flavor of chai tea,
they'll enjoy this icy cold drink.*

**Yield: 3 servings
(about 8 ounces each)**

• • • • • • •

2 cups chai tea, cooled

¹/₂ cup rice milk

1 tablespoon honey or
brown rice syrup

4–6 ice cubes

1. Place all the ingredients in a blender.

2. Blend on medium speed about 1 minute or until the ice cubes are well crushed.

3. Serve immediately.

Strawberry-Orange Super Slushie

Although most kids like sipping this icy drink through a straw, it's thick enough to enjoy with a spoon.

1. Place the strawberries and juice in a blender.

2. Blend on high speed about 1 minute or until the mixture is smooth.

3. Serve immediately.

Yield: 3 servings
(about 8 ounces each)
• • • • • • •

2 pints fresh strawberries
(about 5 cups), hulled
and frozen*

$^1/_2$ cup orange juice

* If using fresh strawberries
that aren't frozen, add about
6 ice cubes.

Pomegranate Hibiscus Tea Cooler

Similar in flavor to cranberries, hibiscus herbal tea is blended with the juice of pomegranates—a superfood known for its healthful benefits—in this refreshing drink. We prefer using herbal tea because it's caffeine-free.

1. Steep the tea bags in the boiling water about 5 minutes. Remove the bags and pour the tea into a pitcher.

2. Add the cold water and pomegranate juice and stir well. Refrigerate about 2 hours or until ice cold.

3. Serve as is or over ice cubes. Garnish with a lemon wedge.

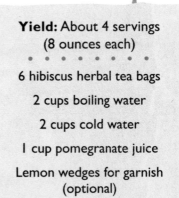

Yield: About 4 servings
(8 ounces each)
• • • • • • • •

6 hibiscus herbal tea bags

2 cups boiling water

2 cups cold water

1 cup pomegranate juice

Lemon wedges for garnish
(optional)

Metric Conversion Tables

COMMON LIQUID CONVERSIONS

Measurement	=	Milliliters
$\frac{1}{4}$ teaspoon	=	1.25 milliliters
$\frac{1}{2}$ teaspoon	=	2.50 milliliters
$\frac{3}{4}$ teaspoon	=	3.75 milliliters
1 teaspoon	=	5.00 milliliters
1 $\frac{1}{4}$ teaspoons	=	6.25 milliliters
1 $\frac{1}{2}$ teaspoons	=	7.50 milliliters
1 $\frac{3}{4}$ teaspoons	=	8.75 milliliters
2 teaspoons	=	10.0 milliliters
1 tablespoon	=	15.0 milliliters
2 tablespoons	=	30.0 milliliters

Measurement	=	Liters
$\frac{1}{4}$ cup	=	0.06 liters
$\frac{1}{2}$ cup	=	0.12 liters
$\frac{3}{4}$ cup	=	0.18 liters
1 cup	=	0.24 liters
1 $\frac{1}{4}$ cups	=	0.30 liters
1 $\frac{1}{2}$ cups	=	0.36 liters
2 cups	=	0.48 liters
2 $\frac{1}{2}$ cups	=	0.60 liters
3 cups	=	0.72 liters
3 $\frac{1}{2}$ cups	=	0.84 liters
4 cups	=	0.96 liters
4 $\frac{1}{2}$ cups	=	1.08 liters
5 cups	=	1.20 liters
5 $\frac{1}{2}$ cups	=	1.32 liters

CONVERTING FAHRENHEIT TO CELSIUS

Fahrenheit	=	Celsius
200–205	=	95
220–225	=	105
245–250	=	120
275	=	135
300–305	=	150
325–330	=	165
345–350	=	175
370–375	=	190
400–405	=	205
425–430	=	220
445–450	=	230
470–475	=	245
500	=	260

CONVERSION FORMULAS

LIQUID		
When You Know	Multiply By	To Determine
teaspoons	5.0	milliliters
tablespoons	15.0	milliliters
fluid ounces	30.0	milliliters
cups	0.24	liters
pints	0.47	liters
quarts	0.95	liters

WEIGHT		
When You Know	Multiply By	To Determine
ounces	28.0	grams
pounds	0.45	kilograms

RESOURCES

For those living with food allergies, the following resources can be invaluable. Along with a list of organizations that offer timely information and support, there are helpful websites, recommended products, and reliable manufacturers that support an allergen-free lifestyle. It is important to note that this list of resources, although extensive, is not complete. Networking and Internet searches will help you discover additional sites, products, and organizations—both established and new.

ORGANIZATIONS

American Academy of Allergy, Asthma & Immunology (AAAAI)
555 East Wells Street, Suite 1100
Milwaukee, WI 53202-3823
414-272-6071
www.aaaai.org
This worldwide organization of medical specialists and healthcare professionals is dedicated to "advancement of the knowledge and practice of allergy, asthma, and immunology for optimal patient care."

American Academy of Pediatrics (AAP)
141 Northwest Point Boulevard
Elk Grove Village, IL 60007-1098
847-434-4000
www.aap.org
"Dedicated to the Health of All Children" is the motto of this organization of pediatricians. Contact them for information on all issues relating to children's health. Also provides doctor referrals.

Anaphylaxis Canada
2005 Sheppard Avenue East, Suite 800
Toronto, Ontario M2J 5B4
Canada
416-785-5666
866-785-5660
www.anaphylaxis.org
This non-profit organization was created by and for people with anaphylaxis. Among its many functions, Anaphylaxis Canada provides information and support for people with this hypersensitivity, helping them lead safe, normal lives.

Asthma and Allergy Foundation of America (AAFA)
8201 Corporate Drive, Suite 1000
Landover, MD 200785
800-7-ASTHMA (800-727-8462)
www.aafa.org
Founded in 1953, this not-for-profit organization is dedicated to improving the quality of life for people with asthma and allergic diseases through education, advocacy, and research. It provides practical information, community-based services, and support to patients and families.

Food Allergy and Anaphylaxis Network (FAAN)
11781 Lee Jackson Highway, Suite 160
Fairfax, VA 22033-3309
800-929-4040
703-691-3179
www.foodallergy.org

To be a world leader in food allergy and anaphylaxis awareness is the goal of this organization. FAAN's many accomplishments include its involvement in legislation regarding historic food labeling, and its educational programs that are taught in schools throughout the United States.

Food Allergy Initiative (FAI)

515 Madison Avenue, Suite 1912
New York, NY 10022-5403
855-FAI-9604 (855-324-9604)
www.foodallergyinitiative.org
The goal of this organization—founded by concerned parents and grandparents—is to build a strong national presence for the food allergy community with the ultimate goal of increased funding for food allergy research.

Institute for Responsible Technology (IRT)

PO Box 469
Fairfield, IA 52556
641-209-1765
www.responsibletechnology.org
The IRT is a world leader in educating policy makers and the public about the health, environmental, agricultural, and economic risks of genetically modified (GM) foods and crops.

HELPFUL WEBSITES

AllergicChild.com

Created by the parents of a severely food allergic child, this site offers information, shared experiences, and practical advice to help keep your food-allergic child safe and healthy while living a full life. Offers free monthly newsletter.

AllergyKids.com

This foundation, whose goal is to protect and restore the "health of loved ones" offers information on the hidden dangers in our food supply and the connection to conditions such as allergies, autism, asthma, and ADHD.

AllergyMoms.com

Started by the mother of a child with multiple food allergies, this website offers coaching sessions for moms and other caregivers, as well as a free newsletter with informative articles, allergy-friendly recipes, and parenting tips.

BabyandKidAllergies.com

This site provides information and links to all things related to allergies, including testing of, recipes for, products for, and much more.

CybelePascal.com

On this site, Cybele Pascal, noted author and mother of a food-allergic family, shares her favorite recipes, as well as tips on new allergen-free products and tidbits from her life as part of a food allergic family.

Dermae.com

This natural skin care line includes products for treating allergic skin reactions.

FoodAllergyKitchen.com

The moderator of this website, which presents extensive allergen-free recipes in all food categories, is the mother of two children with multiple food allergies. The site has been noted as one of the ten best resources for individuals with food allergies.

GlutenFree.com

This online resource offers listings of hundreds of brand name gluten-free and wheat-free products, including breads, cakes, cookies, pasta, prepared meals, and more.

GoAllergyFree.com

Created by the mother of two children with food allergies, this site is a "central hub of allergy-related resources," including allergen-free food products, recipes, and cookbooks. You can also search for allergy-friendly grocery stores and bakeries by state. Its interactive discussion board allows you to post questions, as well as share recipes, product reviews, dining suggestions, etc. with others.

GoDairyFree.org
This informational website offers tips, recipes, and practical advice for those living with milk allergies or lactose intolerance.

HealthyChildren.org
This website, backed by the American Academy of Pediatrics, offers reliable, current healthcare information and guidance for parents and caregivers. Includes information on pediatric allergists—their training, the treatment they provide, and how to locate one.

KidsWithFoodAllergies.org
Designed for families raising children with food allergies, this site offers practical information on such topics as reading food labels and making safe food substitutions. It also presents an extensive collection of recipes that are searchable by category and hosts the Parents of Food Allergic Kids (POFAK)—the largest online support group for families raising food-allergic children.

LocalHarvest.org
Check this site for a directory of farmers' markets, family farms, and other sources of sustainably grown food in your area.

PeanutAllergy.com
This informative site provides helpful tips, key advice, and links to a host of resources on living with a peanut allergy. Through its forums, you can connect with others to share stories, struggles, and successes. Includes a database of peanut- and nut-free products. Find foods, restaurants, recipes, and much more.

TriumphDining.com
Triumph Dining has "developed the most comprehensive gluten-free restaurant guide in North America." It also has a gluten-free grocery guide, as well as special dining cards to help order gluten-free in restaurants. The cards are available in ten languages and tailored to each ethnic cuisine. Offers a free biweekly newsletter with gluten-free recipes, product reviews, and special deals.

waFEAST.org
Washington FEAST (Food Allergy, Eczema, Asthma, and Support Team) is a non-profit advocacy group. Its mission is to educate and support individuals and caregivers who are affected by life-threatening food allergies, and who may also deal with atopic disorders like eczema, and asthma.

BRAND NAME PRODUCTS

Amy's
707-568-4500
www.amyskitchen.com
Frozen vegetarian meals; canned beans, soups, and chilis. Includes varieties that cater to those with food allergies or who have other special dietary needs.

Arrowhead Mills
800-434-4246
www.arrowheadmills.com
Extensive selection of organic baking products, including gluten-free flours and baking mixes, grains, seeds, and beans.

Authentic Foods
800-806-4737
www.authenticfoods.com
Gluten-free flours and baking mixes for bread, cookies, brownies, pizza and pie crusts, pancakes, and more.

Bob's Red Mill
800-349-2173
www.bobsredmill.com
Full line of gluten-free products, including flours and meals; cereals; mixes for breads, cookies, cakes, pancakes, and pizza dough—all produced in a dedicated facility free from wheat and other gluten-containing grains or derivatives.

Daiya
www.daiyafoods.com
Vegan mozzarella, cheddar, and pepperjack cheese varieties that are made without soy, dairy, gluten, egg, peanuts, and tree nuts.

Ener-G
800-331-5222
www.ener-g.com
Gluten-free, wheat-free, dairy-free, nut-free, and kosher-certified products, including Egg Replacer; cookies, cakes, breads; crackers and snacks; and rice pastas.

Enjoy Life Foods
847-260-0300
888-50-ENJOY (888-503-6569)
www.enjoylifefoods.com
Gluten-free, dairy-free, peanut-free, tree-nut free, soy-free, egg-free, and casein-free cookies, cereals, granolas, snack bars, trail mixes, chocolate bars and chips.

Hol-Grain
800-551-3245
www.holgrain.com
Rice products from America's oldest working rice mill. Wheat-free/gluten-free rice crackers and baking mixes; "bread" crumbs made of 100% brown rice.

Ian's Natural Foods
800-54-FOODS (800-543-6637)
www.iansnaturalfoods.com
*Allergy-friendly meals, snacks, and sides that appeal to kids—Alphatots (potatoes shaped like letters); pizza; chicken nuggets, patties, and tenders; mac and **no** cheese; French toast sticks; and more.*

Imagine Foods
800-434-4246
www.tastethedream.com
Rice Dream organic natural beverages; Rice Dream frozen desserts.

Lundberg Family Farms
530-538-3500
www.lundberg.com
Extensive line of certified organic and eco-farmed whole grain rice varieties, blends, and products, including rice cakes, chips, flours, and brown rice syrup.

Maple Grove Farms of Vermont
www.maplegrove.com
Pure maple syrup, maple sugar, and maple sugar candies; gluten-free pancake and waffle mix.

No Nuttin' Foods
866-714-5411
www.nonuttin.com
Gluten-free, peanut-free, nut-free, and dairy-free granola bars and snacks.

NOW foods
888-669-3663
www.nowfoods.com
Agave nectar, date sugar, organic pure maple syrup and brown rice syrup.

Quinoa Corporation
310-217-8125
www.quinoa.net
Ancient Harvest brand organic, gluten/GMO-free quinoa grain, flour, flakes, and pastas. Food Merchant brand ready-made gluten/GMO-free corn polenta.

SunGold Foods
800-437-5539
www.sunbutter.com
SunButter spread—a peanut butter alternative made from sunflower seeds.

Index

JUICE ALIVE
The Ultimate Guide to Juicing Remedies
SECOND EDITION
Steven Bailey, ND, and Larry Trivieri, Jr.

The world of fresh juices offers a powerhouse of antioxidants, vitamins, minerals, and enzymes. The trick is knowing which juices can best serve your needs. In this easy-to-use guide, health experts Dr. Steven Bailey and Larry Trivieri, Jr. tell you everything you need to know to maximize the benefits and tastes of juice.

The book begins with a look at the history of juicing. It then examines the many components that make fresh juice truly good for you—good for weight loss and so much more. Next, it offers practical advice about the types of juices available, as well as buying and storing tips for produce. The second half of the book begins with an important chart that matches up common ailments with the most appropriate juices, followed by over 100 delicious juice recipes. Let *Juice Alive* introduce you to a world bursting with the incomparable tastes and benefits of fresh juice.

$14.95 • 272 pages • 6 x 9-inch quality paperback • ISBN 978-0-7570-0266-3

WHAT YOU MUST KNOW ABOUT VITAMINS, MINERALS, HERBS & MORE
Choosing the Nutrients That Are Right for You
Pamela Wartian Smith, MD, MPH

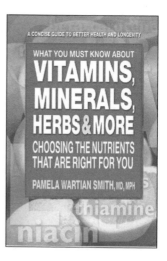

Almost 75 percent of your health and life expectancy is based on lifestyle, environment, and nutrition. Yet even if you follow a sound diet, you are probably not getting all the nutrients you need to prevent disease. In *What You Must Know About Vitamins, Minerals, Herbs & More,* Dr. Pamela Smith explains how you can restore and maintain health through the wise use of nutrients.

Part One of this easy-to-use guide discusses the individual nutrients necessary for good health. Part Two offers personalized nutritional programs for people with a wide variety of health concerns. People without prior medical problems can look to Part Three for their supplementation plans. Whether you want to maintain good health or you are trying to overcome a medical condition, *What You Must Know About Vitamins, Minerals, Herbs & More* can help you make the best choices for the well-being of you and your family.

$15.95 • 448 pages • 6 x 9-inch quality paperback • ISBN 978-0-7570-0233-5

THE WHOLE FOODS ALLERGY COOKBOOK
Two Hundred Gourmet & Homestyle Recipes for the Food Allergic Family
SECOND EDITION
Cybele Pascal

The Whole Foods Allergy Cookbook is the first cookbook to eliminate all eight allergens responsible for 90 percent of food allergies. Each and every dish offered is free of dairy, eggs, wheat, soy, peanuts, tree nuts, fish, and shellfish. You'll find tempting recipes for breakfast pancakes, breads, and cereals; lunch soups, salads, spreads, and sandwiches; dinner entrées and side dishes; dessert puddings, cupcakes, cookies, cakes, and pies; and even after-school snacks ranging from trail mix to pizza and pretzels. Included is a resource guide to organizations that can supply information and support, as well as a shopping guide for hard-to-find items.

If you thought that allergies meant missing out on nutrition, variety, and flavor, think again. With *The Whole Foods Allergy Cookbook* you'll have both the wonderful taste you want and the radiant health you deserve.

$18.95 • 240 pages • 8 x 10-inch quality paperback • ISBN 978-1-890612-45-0

VICKI'S VEGAN KITCHEN
Eating with Sanity, Compassion & Taste
Vicki Chelf

Vegan dishes are healthy, delicious, and surprisingly easy to make. Yet many people are daunted by the idea of preparing meals that contain no animal products. For them, and for everyone who loves great food, chef Vicki Chelf presents a comprehensive cookbook designed to take the mystery out of meatless meals.

Vicki begins by offering tips for making nutritious food choices, as well as an extensive glossary of ingredients. She then discusses the simple kitchen equipment you need to have on hand and explains basic cooking techniques. Following this are twelve chapters packed with over 375 recipes for delicious dips, scrumptious soups, pleasing pastas, decadent desserts, and much, much more. Whether you're interested in compassionate cooking, you value the benefits of a meat-free diet, or you just want to treat your family to a wonderful meal, *Vicki's Vegan Kitchen* will bring delectable vegan fare to your kitchen table.

$17.95 • 320 pages • 7.5 x 9-inch quality paperback • ISBN 978-0-7570-0251-9

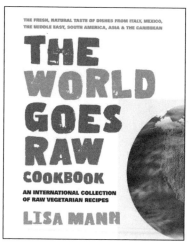

THE WORLD GOES RAW COOKBOOK
An International Collection of Raw Vegetarian Recipes
Lisa Mann

People everywhere know that meals prepared without heat can taste great and improve their overall health. Yet raw cuisine cookbooks have always offered little variety—until now. In *The World Goes Raw Cookbook,* raw food chef Lisa Mann provides a fresh approach to (un)cooking with recipes that have an international twist.

After discussing the healthfulness of a raw food diet, *The World Goes Raw Cookbook* tells you how to stock your kitchen with the tools and ingredients that make it easy to prepare raw meals. What follows are six recipe chapters, each focused on a different ethnic cuisine, including Italian, Mexican, Middle Eastern, Asian, Caribbean, and South American dishes. Whether you are already interested in raw food or are exploring it for the first time, the taste-tempting recipes in *The World Goes Raw Cookbook* can add variety to your life while helping you feel healthier and more energized than ever before.

$16.95 • 176 pages • 7.5 x 9-inch quality paperback • ISBN 978-0-7570-0320-2

EAT SMART, EAT RAW
Creative Vegetarian Recipes for a Healthier Life
Kate Wood

As the popularity of raw vegetarian cuisine continues to soar, so does the evidence that uncooked food is amazingly good for you. From lowering cholesterol to eliminating excess weight, the health benefits of this diet are too important to ignore. Now there is another reason to go raw—taste! In *Eat Smart, Eat Raw,* cook and health writer Kate Wood not only explains how to get started, but also provides kitchen-tested recipes guaranteed to delight even the fussiest of eaters.

Eat Smart, Eat Raw begins by discussing the basics of cooking without heat. This is followed by twelve chapters offering 150 recipes for truly exceptional dishes, including hearty breakfasts, savory soups, satisfying entrées, and luscious desserts. There's even a chapter on the "almost raw." Whether you are an ardent vegetarian or just someone in search of a great meal, *Eat Smart, Eat Raw* may forever change the way you look at an oven.

$15.95 • 184 pages • 7.5 x 9-inch quality paperback • ISBN 978-0-7570-0261-8